# TEACHING GYMNASTICS

# TEACHING GYMNASTICS

### E. Mauldon
*Principal Lecturer in Physical Education,*
*City of Leeds and Carnegie College of Education, Leeds*

### J. Layson
*Principal Lecturer in Physical Education,*
*Anstey College of Physical Education, Sutton Coldfield*

MACDONALD & EVANS LTD
8 John Street, London W.C.1
1965

First published September 1965
Reprinted February 1966
Reprinted July 1966
Reprinted November 1966
Reprinted June 1968
Reprinted May 1969
Reprinted August 1970

©

MACDONALD AND EVANS LTD
1965

S.B.N: 7121 2001 7

PRINTED IN GREAT BRITAIN BY
UNWIN BROTHERS LIMITED
WOKING AND LONDON
(HL7172)

# PREFACE

To some the title of this book would mean more if it were "Modern Educational Gymnastics." It is felt unnecessary, however, to qualify the word gymnastics as this type of work is taught today in most Primary and Secondary schools, and "modern" and "educational" are implied in the term "gymnastics" as used in this text.

The book is intended to help all those interested in teaching the subject; not only the specialist but also the Primary teacher, whose responsibility is perhaps the greater.

Since teaching cannot be learned from a book, if this text is to be of value it must be used practically and adapted to the needs of individual classes. The suggestions are intended as possible starting points and it should be realised that this is not the only way to teach gymnastics. The successful teacher finds his own method of presenting material through a process of experimenting and using his accumulated experience.

Help is given first in the organisation and division of a lesson, including general teaching points which must be considered if the material is to be of any value. Chapters concerned with specific themes or movement ideas are subdivided under the following headings:

(a) *Material*, where the relevant fundamentals of movement are defined and discussed to provide teachers with the foundation of a sound knowledge of movement principles.

(b) *Teaching*, based on practical experience and concerned with methods of introducing and helping children to develop work on the particular idea considered in (a).

(c) *Apparatus*, where the principles of selection and arrangement are discussed and suggestions put forward for provision relative to the theme. It is hoped that these will stimulate teachers to consider the setting of apparatus and tasks thoughtfully and imaginatively. A key to the illustrated apparatus will be found on the following page.

In sections (b) and (c) specific reference has been made, wherever practical, to work considered suitable for Junior or Secondary children. This has not been done consistently since in certain situations it is applicable to both.

The themes dealt with are not to be confused with Laban's sixteen basic movement themes, although in some cases they are closely related and, throughout this book, movement ideas are based on his principles. The material has been carefully selected to cover all aspects of gymnastic work.

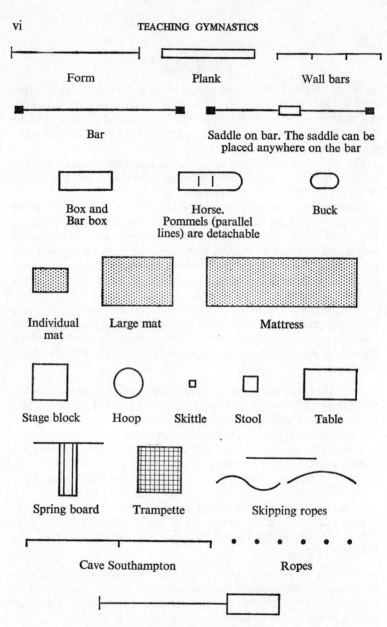

Inclined forms or planks touch apparatus;
*e.g.* inclined form to bar box

Key to symbols used for apparatus illustrated in the text. With minor exceptions the scale employed is $\frac{1}{8}$ in. = 1 ft.

Material has been separated from the teaching as it is necessary for the teacher to have both a depth and breadth of knowledge, only a little of which may be passed on to the children. He must see the subject as a whole, whereas the children will be concerned mainly with their present experience. It is for the teacher to understand the correlation between themes and help his class relate past and present work.

In several chapters reference is made to action tasks and movement tasks. In the former the actions are dictated, *e.g.* "Run and jump over the mat, return by rolling," but the way in which these actions are carried out—slowly, with a one-sided stress or in a particular direction—is left to the child. In the latter a movement task is given, *e.g.* "Travel symmetrically" and the way in which this is carried out—rolling, sliding, jumping—is the choice of each individual.

The decision whether or not to use photographs in a book dealing with movement is a difficult one to make. It is admitted that photographs are of limited value but they are included in those chapters where it is thought they augment the text.

It is also difficult to describe concisely the varied actions which might result from a given challenge. Therefore it has often been necessary to restrict examples to known skills such as handstands. This has obvious disadvantages but such skills are given as recognisable solutions to a task. There will be variations of this particular skill as well as many other inventions. The skills named do not differ substantially from others and have no particular merit as such.

One complete chapter is devoted to movement observation, so essential if teachers are to assess what is needed and develop what is produced. No attempt has been made to pursue a detailed study of movement, and observation has been discussed only inasmuch as it applies to gymnastics and the teaching of gymnastics.

Finally, progressions which might be used as a guide for teaching children between the ages of seven and sixteen are discussed in Chapter 14. It can be only a guide, as the teacher alone knows the children and the circumstances.

June, 1965                                       E. M.
                                                 J. L.

# ACKNOWLEDGMENTS

WE wish to thank both Miss Hutton, headmistress of Lawrence Road Junior School, Liverpool, and Mr. Allen, Headmaster of Totty's Hall Junior School, Crewe, for allowing us to work with and photograph the children in their respective schools. We would also like to acknowledge the help of Miss M. T. Crabbe, C.B.E., M.A., late Principal of I. M. Marsh College of Physical Education, Liverpool, and Miss M. J. P. Laurence, M.A., Principal of Cheshire County Training College, Crewe, whose co-operation made it possible to photograph students' work in their colleges.

Finally we wish to express our thanks to the two photographers, Mr. Ian Sime, B.Sc. and Mr. Don Holstead, B.A. (Cantab.), to Mr. John Allen, who designed the cover, and to the many other friends and colleagues who have given generously of their time to read, discuss and correct the text.

E. M.
J. L.

# CONTENTS

# INTRODUCTION

SINCE the beginning of the century there has been a continuous modification of terminology reflecting the changing attitudes towards what is known today as Physical Education. The most recent, that of "P.T." to "P.E.," indicates a radical change. It would seem that there are two main reasons for this, the first a general broadening of educational thought, and the second the profound influence of Rudolf Laban's work.

In education the concept of the child as an individual is now of prime importance. The teacher no longer aims to teach the hypothetical average of the class, but helps each child to develop and realise his potential. This is a long process in which exploring, experimenting, discovering, repeating, selecting and perfecting have their place. If the approach is to be successful and result in a growing self-confidence, it is essential that the child works at his own pace and level. Along with self-discovery there is an increasing awareness of others and the child learns to adapt himself to social groupings, experiencing the give and take involved.

Leading physical educationists had for some time felt the need to reassess the work, and Laban's discoveries and formulation of principles governing all movement gave them the means by which this could be done.

The word "physical" is misleading in that it implies that the teacher is concerned only with the body. "Education through Movement" or "Movement Education" would be more relevant since the teacher is dealing with children who think, feel and do.

Physical Education covers an increasing range of activities; many schools now include dance, gymnastics, team games and individual sports as well as outdoor pursuits. The latter, a fairly recent addition, involves learning specialised techniques. The traditional games still hold an important place in the curriculum but are being superseded by individual sports. In all games-like activities the stress is on learning specific skills, and although certain allowances are made for individual deviation there is generally a right or a wrong way of performing these skills. Gymnastics is also concerned with skill but in a different sense. Acquisition of skill is not an end in itself but the means by which children can experience and understand movement in a variety of practical situations. In gymnastics the individual is free to invent and select his own answers to a variety of given tasks and so the movement range is wide compared with games and outdoor activities, but it is not comprehensive. Only modern educational dance can cover the complete range of effort and all movement possibilities, since, unlike objective work, it is not restricted to action but involves the experience of movement in a meaningful and creative way.

The aims in teaching gymnastics are:

1. To develop efficiency and a skilled use of the body in practical situations when working alone and with others, on the floor and on apparatus.

2. To stimulate an understanding and appreciation of objective movement coupled with an ability to invent and select appropriate actions.

The teacher endeavours to give valid movement experience by drawing upon the child's natural desire to come to terms with his physical environment. Use is made of the child's innate love of moving, and his natural ease and fluency of movement are retained and developed. That part of movement education which can be accomplished through gymnastics calls into play both thought and action, so that understanding and doing are concurrent. Agility, strength, stamina and poise are not exclusively aimed for but are a valuable outcome of this way of working. It is impossible to claim a complete transference of training from one practical situation to another but it is likely that the skilled gymnast is in a position to profit by his gymnastic experience in related activities such as diving, ski-ing and rock-climbing.

Laban's influence has been mentioned and it is expedient to go into further detail although it is impossible to do justice to his work in this text. There is still much misunderstanding by teachers of the place of the four motion factors, Weight, Space, Time and Flow in Physical Education. It is a disservice to try to remould Laban's ideas or graft them onto well-established physical activities. The motion factors provide a basis for understanding all movement and in Physical Education, with the exception of dance, the stress is on objective function, a part of movement only. Thus it is not a matter of "applying" Weight, Space, Time and Flow to a particular activity but the reverse, that is, appreciating how the activity can be considered in the light of these fundamental principles.

Gymnastics is objective, practical aims being achieved in a skilled way. In their book *Effort* Laban and Lawrence write ". . . skill is acquired through the gradual refinement of the feel of the movement and any training has indeed to promote this feel which, in its essence, is the awakening of the sense for the proportions of motion factors." In answering any given task efficiently each individual will inevitably colour his actions with a personal stress. This will affect the way of moving but not the end result. Gymnastic actions demand specific effort combinations. Certain proportions of the motion factors are stressed and others, though present, are latent.

In functional activities it is the measurable aspect of the motion factors that is important; the movement sensation, significant in expressive situations, exists, but is not developed. Thus, in referring to the Weight factor in gymnastics, it is the degree of energy and bodily tension that is considered. In Space the gymnast is concerned with direction, level, pathway and body shape, while in Time the degrees of speed provide the content. The relevant aspect of the Flow factor is that of control.

The measurable aspects of Weight, Space, Time and Flow together give the substance of gymnastics; but in isolation do not provide gymnastic themes. The teacher is dealing with children who move, with greater or lesser energy and control, through space and in time. Therefore themes are selected which have these ideas integrated although probably one aspect is stressed in a lesson and the others are subordinate.

Many criticisms have been levelled at gymnastics and this is inevitable when new aims, approaches and content are emerging. No doubt the teaching has often been poor—it takes time for those trained along other lines to assimilate and change to different ideas, and this is understandable, for teachers rarely abandon an established method until a new one has proved itself. In addition, the training of teachers in this way has involved much re-thinking and experimenting.

It would be worth while anticipating and answering some of the more repeated criticisms. One that "in modern gymnastics variety is stressed for variety's sake" is voiced by those who see no point in such tasks as "find as many different ways of travelling as you can" or "repeat your actions with changes of speed." Teachers with little understanding probably do stress variety for the wrong reasons. Acquisition of skill is a normal process, part of the business of living; the normality or backwardness of the young child is judged by his skill repertoire. Later there is much personal satisfaction in learning more intricate skills and it is natural that once a skill is mastered it should be played with and repeated. It is this playing with a skill or action that gives complete mastery and inevitably leads to variation and new skills. An inventive child with a certain degree of skill will produce varied work instead of movement clichés or actions habitually strung together. Variety of action or versatility is fostered in gymnastics because it increases general skilfulness and the wider the repertoire the more appropriate can be the choice in objective situations.

Another criticism that "the modern approach is successful in the beginning stages but is incapable of development, so that formal work has to take its place" indicates a lack of movement understanding. The later chapters in this book show the extent of the work. Gymnastics is limited not so much by its nature as by the understanding of the teacher. It is essential that the teacher knows his material and is able to develop it in relation to the needs and ability of his class.

A fault found by some in modern work is that in catering for all the standard is inevitably low or non-existent. Since no common standard is imposed, competition as such does not occur and challenges are worded so that each child may succeed at his own level. However, there is competition in that the child strives to improve his own skill and understanding, but these are in relation to his starting point and ability. Thus the teacher encourages each child to vie with himself and the attitude should be one of, "How can I improve this part of my sequence?" or "Can I get my feet, instead of my knees, onto the high box?" Obviously children are very quick to realise the capabilities of others but normally they accept these without misgiving.

Certainly the teaching of gymnastics requires much more of the teacher than formerly. He must understand and be sympathetic towards his children, have a sound movement knowledge and be able to observe. The results of good teaching are to be seen in confident, skilful movers and inventive, lively work. Moreover, the fun of producing something which is "mine" and the excitement and satisfaction of working with others has an educational value not to be ignored.

# CHAPTER 1

# LESSON PLAN AND ORGANISATION

WHEN planning a lesson, the space, equipment and the time available have all to be considered as well as the age and aptitude of the class. The space varies from playground or hall to a fully equipped gymnasium. Some schools are well supplied with a variety of small and large apparatus both fixed and portable, while others are limited to small apparatus. The time allocated could be from twenty minutes in some Junior schools to forty-five minutes in some Secondary schools. It is realised that this time is often shortened when Juniors, for example, have to be assembled and led to the playground or when apparatus has to be collected from other classrooms. Similarly in the Secondary school, children may arrive in small groups having travelled from other parts of the building. In both Junior and Secondary schools time has often to be allowed for complete changing and showering. The teacher, with all these considerations in mind, will plan his lesson accordingly.

It is advisable to outline a series of lessons around a particular theme selected with the specific needs of the class in mind. It should be noted, however, that although one main theme will be developed, related subsidiary themes will naturally be referred to. Each lesson in turn can then be planned in more detail, building on the teacher's observation and the results of previous work.

Whatever the length of lesson, the proportion of time allocated to floor and apparatus work has to be considered. The amount of time actually spent moving can be divided in the ratio $\frac{2}{3}:\frac{1}{3}$, $\frac{1}{2}:\frac{1}{2}$, $\frac{1}{3}:\frac{2}{3}$. When introducing a new idea the time spent working at floor level will be greater than that on apparatus—$\frac{2}{3}:\frac{1}{3}$, but in consecutive lessons the working time will probably be equally divided—$\frac{1}{2}:\frac{1}{2}$. Once the particular theme has been fully explored at floor level the children will need a greater proportion of time to exploit the possibilities on apparatus—$\frac{1}{3}:\frac{2}{3}$.

Floor work will consist of limbering and movement training, while apparatus may include work with small equipment, with a partner, in a group or on large apparatus.

## FLOOR WORK

### Limbering

This is a dual preparation of body and mind. The need to prepare the body for the vigorous, energetic movements which follow later

1

in the lesson is obvious, whereas the mental preparation is often neglected.

In the Junior school, where children are naturally active and where other lessons involve moving about the classroom, the need to prepare physically is not so necessary. In the Secondary school, however, where children spend most of their day immobile in desks and are less inclined to physical activity, it is essential that the body is brought to a state of readiness.

In both Junior and Secondary schools the need for mental preparation should not be overlooked. In other lessons although movement may be involved in the activity, whether this be Drama, Music or Art, the focus is not on moving. Once inside the hall or gymnasium the child is expected to think in movement terms; therefore this brief period at the beginning of the lesson is a useful transition. Complete co-ordination of body and mind must be considered in this introductory stage of the lesson. Movements used in everyday life are, on the whole, automatic, actions rarely being consciously considered. In gymnastics, as the child is no longer directed, the tasks and challenges set by the teacher demand a mental effort and involve selection and decision.

In gymnastics the trunk and limbs are used equally in travelling actions, necessitating the preparation of all body parts to receive weight. Continuity of action should be stressed where movements follow naturally, each influencing the next. This should be done with a gradual increase of speed and energy until, towards the end of the limbering, a climax is reached. In the course of the lesson since the spine will be arched, curled, stretched and twisted, these movements should be experienced on the floor and in flight during limbering. Particular care should be taken to ensure that the trunk is activated and this will result if movements are related to the centre of the body. The preparation of feet and ankles should be stressed, as these are the main ejectors and receivers of weight.

Actions at first will probably be on the spot, but these should quickly develop into travelling. Once locomotion takes place an awareness of the general space is needed; control in speed and changes of direction will be required in order to avoid others also moving within the same area. Judgment and ability to adapt to changing situations is now important and will be stressed in these first few minutes.


## TASKS FOR LIMBERING

As only three or four minutes are devoted to this preparation, a task should be set, the answer to which fulfils a number of limbering requirements.

*Task* 1.—Invent a sequence of bodily actions, *e.g.* run, jump and roll.

*Task* 2.—Explore a series of repetitive actions, *e.g.* rocking, rolling or transferring weight from hands to feet.

*Task* 3.—Experiment with ways of travelling using various methods of weight transference, *e.g.* rolling, sliding, flight or step-like actions.

*Task* 4.—Work close to the ground, travel over the floor and use it to gain height. This task could be related to a familiar theme, in this case variation in level.

*Task* 5.—Work on a variety of actions which start and end on the feet. This task could be the exploratory process of the main theme of the lesson, *e.g.* transference of weight.

*Task* 6.—Practise a sequence begun in a previous lesson. This depends on its suitability; a sequence involving resiliency would require a brief preliminary preparation, whereas a transference of weight sequence could be started immediately.

*Task* 7.—Repeat or recall a sequence particularly enjoyed.

The first few minutes of the lesson, therefore, are particularly valuable, for when the brief periods allocated to movement in some schools are considered, the stress must surely be in making maximum use of the time. Although ideally the class should be trained to begin work as soon as they have finished changing, there are certain circumstances which prevent this. Wherever possible the aim should be to get the children into the habit of moving quickly to the lesson, of changing and beginning purposeful work straight away.

## Movement Training

This part of the lesson begins when the main theme is introduced or the movement idea embarked upon in the previous lesson is re-called and developed. The aim is twofold, for although the teacher is concerned with training bodily skill, he must also attempt to provide the children with an experience which will extend their movement knowledge and understanding. He should realise that floor work is not an end in itself but the simplest way of exploring movement ideas which can then be applied advantageously on apparatus. In formal gymnastics a few selected bodily skills were taught. The training of the body is still one of the main aims but with a wider implication—that of understanding movement through the acquisition of skill. The class should then be expected to use this knowledge and ability appropriately when working in other situations such as with a partner or on apparatus.

When introducing a movement idea, children should be given time

B

to experiment with the task set; and it is during this exploratory period that the teacher must be particularly alert and observe the needs of the class as well as those of individuals.

## AN EXAMPLE OF HELPING THE WHOLE CLASS

The idea that the body can stretch is introduced and the class may first respond by stretching while standing on their feet or lying on the ground. The teacher could then begin to extend this experience by suggesting that weight is taken on parts other than the feet and give, as an example, shoulders. This is a skill involving inversion most of the class can attempt; a position in which a complete extension of the lower half can be experienced and where the legs are free to reach out and penetrate the surrounding space.

The teacher might suggest that a stretch can be achieved while the body is in flight, as in leaping or in a catspring-like action. These ideas need not all be given at once; the first suggestion may be sufficient and the class left to discover other possibilities. The amount of help the class needs as a whole must be left to the teacher's discretion.

## EXAMPLES OF HELPING INDIVIDUALS

This may be done in many ways and only a few are listed below.

A child may need assistance in *clarifying* his particular movement, *e.g.* he may be working at the task of taking weight on many parts of the body and experimenting with weight on shoulders. The teacher may draw his attention to the fact that he is supporting himself not only on shoulders but also using the upper part of the arm, and may suggest that he lessen the area of support, thus taking all his weight on shoulders alone.

Another child may need to be *urged to greater effort*. This requires keen observation on the part of the teacher, to distinguish between one child who is working to the best of his ability, and another who perhaps is an able mover but lazy, and is producing work below that of which he is capable. The teacher should also learn to recognise the child who constantly underestimates his ability and needs *reassuring*.

Some children will certainly be stimulated to greater effort, and experience a true sense of achievement when *praised* for their contribution to the lesson.

The able child may need *further challenges* or ideas to help him produce work comparable with his ability. It may be suggested that he include a greater variety, perhaps lengthening the sequence.

The child whose ability is limited may require further help, and with *encouragement* will produce a sequence, simple yet well planned, which will both satisfy the performer and fulfil the task set.

The teacher should be completely familiar with his movement material and realise that the less able and less inventive his class, the more he may be required to take the lead in the exploratory period, introducing a few new ideas at a time. With a more imaginative class it may only be individuals who need specific help.

## APPARATUS WORK

With the two aspects of floor work completed, the next part of the lesson can now begin: work with or on apparatus, small and large, or work with partners or groups. The time allowed for apparatus work should include that taken to erect and clear it away. Therefore organisation should be such that the minimum amount of time is taken on grouping and the handling and placement of apparatus.

Throughout the rest of this chapter the work is dealt with separately for the Junior and Secondary schools, as variations in type of equipment used, space available and requirements of each age group are so great. The Secondary teacher, however, who is beginning gymnastics with first years will find much material in the Junior section applicable to his work, just as the Junior teacher who is responsible for a class over a period of years will be able to use some of the suggestions dealt with in the Secondary section.

### JUNIOR

### *Grouping*

When children come into the Junior school they have rarely worked in set groups. Infant groupings are naturally constantly changing and children wander freely from one piece of apparatus to another. In the Junior school the child will eventually be expected to work with others on a set piece of apparatus, to help erect and clear away, handling it carefully and safely. He will have to learn to share apparatus, to take his turn, to help others and to remain with the same group for perhaps as long as half a term. All this needs careful and consistent training and should be introduced gradually. When a class is ready to work in small groups the teacher could use the following progression as a means of arriving at work in fours. It is realised that this may take as long as a term if the class has only one period a week. Tasks on the apparatus will vary, however, and, if the children are kept fully occupied exploring new movement ideas, the time will not be wasted.

*Lessons* 1–2.—All work with individual mats.
*Lessons* 3–4.—All work with individual hoops.
*Lessons* 5–6.—Half the class work with mats and half with hoops, changing over within the lesson.

*Lessons* 7–10.—Half the class collect a mat and the other half a
hoop, each child finds a partner and both work with the mat and
hoop, arranged in a way the teacher feels appropriate.

*Lessons* 11–14.—The two may work with a mat and hoop plus
another piece of small apparatus, *e.g.* a rope, two skittles and a
cane, a chair or a stool.

From this point onwards a combination of two groups will produce
groups of four with two hoops, two mats, stool and skittles available,
which if carefully placed could provide a challenging situation for
seven- or eight-year olds.

Once children have had the experience of working in fours or
fives, different groupings can be attempted, *e.g.* if apparatus is used
which involves height, children of similar size may be required to
work together, whereas if partner work is being introduced the teacher may decide to allow friends to work with each other.

In the lower Junior school, boys and girls mix freely in classroom
activities as well as in the hall or playground and, where this continues
throughout the school, they work together naturally on apparatus.
In this situation, each contributes towards an appreciation of the
others' qualities of movement, the girls "catching" some of the speed
and dash of the boys' movements, the boys assimilating the finish
and precision of the girls'. This may not be the case in all schools and
teachers may feel that at a certain age Junior boys have preferences
not held by girls of the same age and arrange groups and apparatus
accordingly.

## Handling of Apparatus

When children are first introduced to work with apparatus, the
teacher should insist that the equipment is handled with care. Children, on the whole, will respond and take a pride in doing a job well,
and can be most precise when this is demanded. Apparatus trolleys
and containers, well labelled, help to keep the apparatus tidy and
general preservation of valuable equipment can be engendered.

## Organisation of Apparatus

Organisation of apparatus before the lesson can sometimes reduce
the amount of time taken in setting it up. In lessons where small
apparatus is used it can be placed in piles around the hall or playground, avoiding confusion when children collect equipment, and
allowing the pace of the lesson to be maintained. Where several
pieces of small equipment are to be used by each group, they can
be placed near the area of erection. This could be done by a few

children before the lesson begins, or the teacher himself could distribute the apparatus while the children are limbering.

The introduction of several pieces of apparatus can be organised in different ways. The simplest of these is to keep the apparatus the same for all:

**Apparatus**—individual mat, a rope and two hoops.

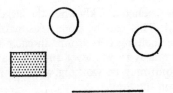

One progression from this is to use the same apparatus but to rearrange it slightly for each group.

**Apparatus**—as before.

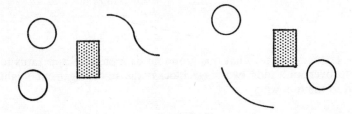

Another progression is for half the class to work with the same apparatus while the other half works with different apparatus, *e.g.* with a class of forty, divided into ten groups of four, five groups could work with apparatus (*a*), and the other five with apparatus (*b*).

**Apparatus** (*a*)—individual mat, a rope and a hoop.

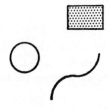

**Apparatus** (*b*)—individual mat, two ropes, skittle.

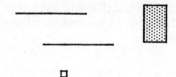

The next stage is reached quickly when the larger pieces of apparatus are introduced. This can be done reasonably simply in three lessons, the teacher helping two groups in each lesson to add their large piece of apparatus to whatever small apparatus they may be using, *e.g.* one group may be working with the mat and hoop and two ropes placed on the floor.

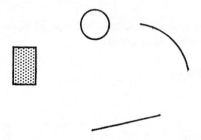

The teacher may feel that this group needs a piece of apparatus to jump over and adds two stage blocks; the re-arrangement might lead to the following:

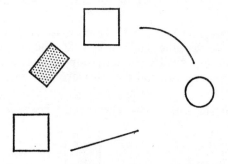

This simple re-arrangement will not take long and the teacher could easily deal with the introduction of two new sets of apparatus in one lesson. Therefore, after three lessons, six new arrangements will be completed.

Once more complicated apparatus is arranged, speed of erection has to be considered. All the apparatus may have to be collected from the same store room, in which case the children setting up apparatus farthest away from the store cupboard should be allowed to collect their apparatus first, arrange it and begin work, once the teacher has checked for safety. Whenever possible each group should erect and put away the same apparatus for several weeks; having worked on other pieces they return to put the original away. Thus each child becomes proficient in the handling of one piece of apparatus before learning to deal with something new. This could be referred to as their "home" apparatus and will save valuable time, as, with constant repetition, efficient organisation of handling and placing will result.

Given sufficient training it should be possible for Juniors to erect any apparatus they are going to use, and this should be regarded as an integral part of the lesson. Lifting, lowering and adjusting apparatus with others gives practical experience of manipulating objects; it requires co-operation and can be used to stress the care of apparatus and a sense of responsibility.

With children who have worked in groups for some time on large apparatus, re-arrangements of this can present certain problems. One way of overcoming difficulties in organisation could be to use the "card" system. The group is handed a card on which is clearly marked:

(*a*) the apparatus to be collected,
(*b*) the placement,
(*c*) the task.

A leader can take responsibility for following the instructions, although the group as a whole help arrange the apparatus. The teacher can later stress spacing and more exact placement. When the groups are ready to change over, either the card can be left behind or the leader can remain to explain the task.

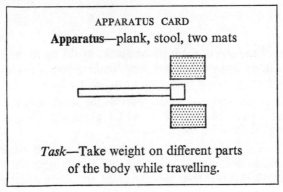

APPARATUS CARD
**Apparatus**—plank, stool, two mats

*Task*—Take weight on different parts
of the body while travelling.

When fixed apparatus is involved, the planning of apparatus has to be organised more carefully. It may be necessary for each group to see the placement of their apparatus in relation to others; therefore a large plan could be made available and placed in the classroom.

In Junior work, when children are so very active and attack each piece of apparatus with renewed vigour, it is essential that individuals should be able to spend the maximum amount of time working on apparatus and the minimum in waiting. Time-wasting queues should therefore be avoided and the following points considered.

## 1. NUMBER IN GROUP

Once children begin to work in groups the numbers should be kept small and the provision of apparatus such that each individual may work continuously with only a brief rest between turns.

## 2. VARIETY OF APPROACH

A variety of approach and pathway should be provided and the teacher should point out that individuals need not adopt the same starting point and that tracks over, under and through apparatus can vary, *e.g.* a group of four can work simultaneously using this apparatus skilfully and avoiding each other.

**Apparatus**—a plank inclined onto a stool and two mats.

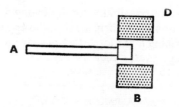

A begins at the end of the inclined plank, works up to the stool and onto the floor, using either mat, and, making use of the floor space when returning, travels back to his original position.

B begins on the mat and works towards the stool, uses it and lands back on his own mat, travels across the plank and back to his own mat using the floor on the return route.

C begins on the floor facing the stool, gets on and off using B's mat as it becomes free, travels from this mat to the other via the floor, works across this mat then uses the plank travelling underneath and over the top, then back up the plank using the stool a second time and back to his starting position.

D begins on the mat and travels diagonally across it, uses the space underneath the inclined plank, travels diagonally across the second mat and then uses the floor space to get to the end of the plank, travels along the plank and uses the stool to land back in his original position.

### 3. SHARING OF APPARATUS

The teacher can help to make the children aware of places where overtaking or passing is possible. They should also understand that apparatus can often be shared and should also appreciate that space around the apparatus can equally well be used. The pattern of working away from and back towards the apparatus should be encouraged, rather than keeping constantly in contact with it.

### 4. RETURN ACTIVITY

A choice of return activity can be given, providing an additional challenge and helping children to use the floor space in an inventive way.

**Apparatus**—a plank inclined to a stool, a mat, four hoops, three ropes.

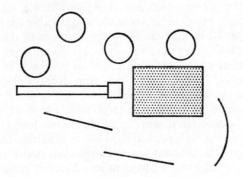

### 5. UTILISATION OF FLOOR SPACE

There should be adequate space surrounding each arrangement, allowing maximum freedom of approach. If this area is kept free and exploited, the apparatus provided could cater for a group of four or five.

**Apparatus**—a table and two mats.

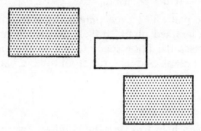

Where space is limited in the hall or playground, it is advisable to provide some groups with normal working space and to limit others, thus allowing at least half the class, in turn, to work with the necessary freedom of unhampered movement.

## Provision of Apparatus

When planning apparatus, thought must be given to providing a variety of situations; wherever possible Juniors should be given opportunity for swinging, climbing, balancing, clearing heights, negotiating small spaces, jumping on and off apparatus, sliding and twisting. Juniors, boys in particular, love to clear obstacles or to run and jump from a height, therefore at least one piece of apparatus should make provision for this type of activity. Where large apparatus is scarce, use can be made of the stage, stage blocks, steps, ammunition boxes and low tables which are strong and stable, while inclined forms or planks attached to stools are also suitable for this activity.

Climbing and swinging are favourite activities of this age group, and this should be remembered when providing apparatus for an energetic Junior class. Few Junior schools possess apparatus which includes hanging ropes but most have some form of climbing frame, and children should be stimulated to use this in a variety of ways. As well as being provided with large spaces to work in, children should also be expected to work in a limited area, learning to control their bodies within that space. Raised hoops or skittles and canes can be used to provide different spaces to get over, under and through. Work with a partner and a hoop can be sufficiently challenging, even for older Juniors, if the teacher and class appreciate the variety of ways a hoop can be held and the number of ways in which it can be used (*see* Chapter on Partner Work).

## Tasks on Apparatus

When setting tasks using individual pieces of apparatus with Juniors who have little or no movement experience, the class needs the security provided by directed work. Children whose movement vocabulary is limited cannot be expected to take advantage of a wide choice. The teacher must give confidence by guiding them carefully and skilfully through the exploratory stages of any theme. One method of helping children over this initial period is to give action tasks. With a class experimenting with ways of travelling, the following tasks could be given:

**Apparatus**—individual mats.

*Task 1.*—Run and jump over your mat lengthways.

*Task 2.*—Run and jump across your mat.

*Task 3.*—Take off from two feet or one foot as you jump.

*Task 4.*—Jump up to your mat and roll across it.

*Task 5.*—Hop from side to side.

*Task 6.*—Run to the mat, jump over it and turn in the air.

The teacher can then challenge the class to find other ways of approaching the mat, and to discover alternative methods of crossing it. Eventually, having been given much freedom, the task can be such that the children are again limited, *e.g.* the teacher may have noted that not many children are attempting to take weight on the hands, therefore the task might be:

*Task 7.*—Using your hands on the mat, make your feet go from side to side.

If the theme of previous lessons has been that of curling and stretching and the class has experimented with travelling keeping the body curled or stretched, then the task on individual mats might be:

*Task 8.*—Approach the mat keeping curled and stretch as you go over the mat.

This shows a possible transition from an action to a movement task.

Having allowed the children a great amount of freedom, the teacher may then set progressive challenges based on the results produced. One might include both movement and action tasks.

*Task 9.*—Roll towards the mat, cross with the body stretched, jump away and turn. Repeat, but this time cross the mat taking weight on a different part of the body.

When each piece of small apparatus has been used in many different ways and the children have built up a considerable movement vocabulary on each, the progression to work with two or three pieces of small apparatus arranged in a circuit will be simple.

When introducing large apparatus for the first time the children need not necessarily be given a task. Time is needed to get the "feel" of it and find ways round, so it will not be until the following lesson that any problems are set.

At first it is usual for the whole class to work on the same task related to the movement idea experienced in previous work on the floor. Once other themes have been introduced, groups can be expected to work at a variety of tasks. It may be possible for the whole class to be working on the same theme, *e.g.* time changes, but stressing different aspects on apparatus—*see* Chapter 7.

Placing and arrangement of apparatus and the setting of subsequent tasks is not a haphazard affair. It requires considerable care, thought and understanding of what each piece and arrangement provides, always relating this to extend the movement experience of the class. Often one sees the same arrangement of apparatus used for a complete term, with different tasks set. This is possible, but all too frequently results in disappointing work with little variety or originality.

In conclusion it should be noted that objective movement plays a large part in the child's life. Children at this age have an abundance of energy and the need for regular activity is very great. Gymnastic work should be seen in the light of the needs of this age group, and apparatus and tasks must always relate to their movement characteristics.

## SECONDARY

### *Grouping*

Children in the Junior school have all shared apparatus and worked with others, therefore at Secondary level the process of grouping does not provide such a problem. Thought should be given, however, to the composition of groups of children, which may vary according to the theme of the lesson. Groups of friends can work together in the early stages, but once bars, for example, are introduced it may be necessary to re-arrange groups according to height. If partner work is being explored, again the teacher may allow friends to work together at first, but later it is advisable to change partners. Other such considerations are dealt with in the Chapter on Partner Work.

The teacher should realise that it is limiting to allow children always to work in the same group and he should ensure that those of similar ability are not always together.

### *Handling of Apparatus*

Accepting the fact that children in the first year at Secondary school will have come from a variety of Junior schools where the movement experience and equipment used will have differed widely, it is best to assume that most of the fixed and portable apparatus will be new to the majority. It should therefore be the policy to introduce this gradually, with every child learning to handle each piece of apparatus safely and efficiently.

First years can be taught quickly how to carry mats and forms, with special reference made to mats that must not be folded and attention drawn to mat handles, which should be used. The two children carrying forms should realise that each has a responsibility for the other, and that they should both be alert and aware of other children who may move across their path. Care should be taken to draw attention to the placement of mats so that they neither overlap nor produce gaps when placed together. When mats are used for landing purposes the class should be made aware of the need to place them sensibly in relation to the task.

Reasonably soon the class can be shown how to get out hanging ropes, as this is the easiest piece of fixed apparatus to manipulate. Wheeled apparatus also could be handled and stabilised. This will include in most modern gymnasia a box, buck and horse; but when these pieces are not mobile then the children should be helped to carry them efficiently and this will include carrying layers of the box. In most cases first years should not be expected to work on the full box and so the dismantling of this piece of apparatus must be covered even with certain wheeled types. Time spent in this early stage in training children to handle apparatus is certainly not wasted, in fact much time and anxiety will be saved later in the year, when the teacher feels secure in the knowledge that any apparatus can be handled efficiently and safely by any child in the class.

Apparatus such as bars, window ladders or hinged wall sections which involve uprights, wedges and pegs should be dealt with most carefully. The whole class should be shown how the apparatus works and should be taught the correct order of movements. The appropriate number of children can then be selected to get this apparatus out and put it away for the next few weeks. Each new piece which is introduced should only be erected in order that the group can use it; there seems little point in getting out apparatus only to put it away again.

By the end of the first term the children between them should be able to handle every available piece of apparatus with the exception of trampettes and spring boards. By the end of the first year every child in the class should be able to handle any piece of apparatus. The class should also be made aware of apparatus that needs checking during the period of work, e.g. they should realise that pegs and wedges may work loose, that mats may become displaced and that hooks on inclined forms need to be checked from time to time. The teacher, however, should undertake the ultimate responsibility for the safe erection and placing of apparatus.

## Organisation of Apparatus

Various arrangements of mats and forms will suffice as apparatus for the first few weeks. These can be used most effectively and provide challenging situations. With six children in a group, arrangements could be:

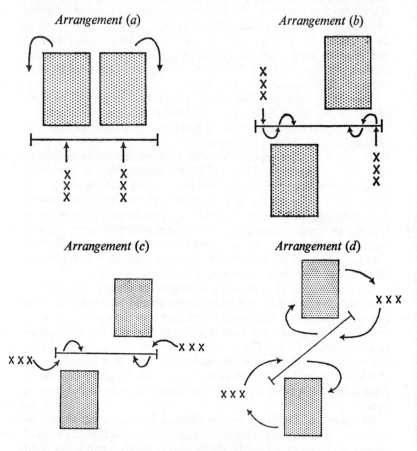

*Arrangement (a)*

*Arrangement (b)*

*Arrangement (c)*

*Arrangement (d)*

As new pieces of apparatus are introduced, *e.g.* bar, horse, ropes, these can be used by three groups of children while the remainder work on a new arrangement of forms and mats. A changeover could then take place during the lesson so that each child has a period of time on apparatus which is familiar as well as on a new piece.

Once the class has learnt to manipulate ropes, box, horse and buck, these pieces can be combined with forms and mats to provide a more challenging situation, and if arranged carefully can help the children explore the many and varied approaches towards, and pathways over, the apparatus. Where the top layers of the box only are being used, in some types the lower ones can also be utilised with forms inclined either broadways or lengthways on.

Forms will usually suggest ways of approach and mats provide landing areas, therefore if apparatus is placed in a straight line the results will be limited, whereas in the following arrangements a variety of starting points and tracks present themselves.

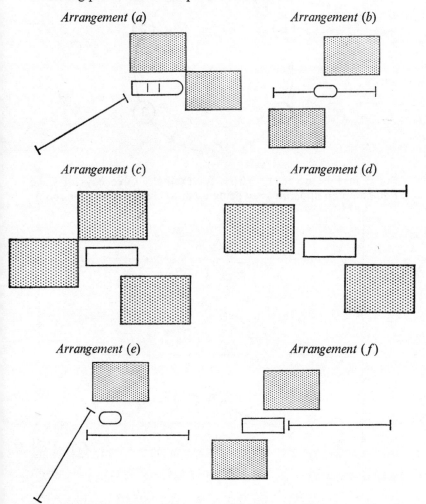

*Arrangement (a)*          *Arrangement (b)*

*Arrangement (c)*          *Arrangement (d)*

*Arrangement (e)*          *Arrangement (f)*

As with Junior classes, groups should set up and put away their "home" piece of apparatus for several lessons, becoming familiar with this and saving valuable time.

Each group should be given at least one change of apparatus each lesson and care should be taken to see that the selection of consecutive pieces varies. This will ensure that heaving is not followed by swinging, nor will work which includes a box immediately precede a similar arrangement with the horse. The usual method of change-over is to rotate thus:

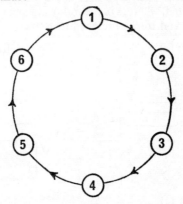

but it may be necessary where, for example, three bays of Cave Southampton apparatus are being used, to change across the room:

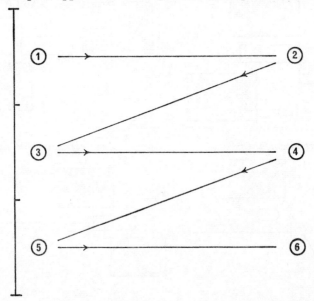

## Provision of Apparatus

Apparatus should not only provide obstacles for the children to negotiate but also be considered from the point of view that it creates spaces. Narrow and wide surfaces should be provided, as well as flat, tipped and rounded areas. Height and length can vary considerably as children become more expert in judging distances, and opportunity should be given to work on angled and asymmetrical obstacles.

Forms, although used in isolation in the elementary stages of gymnastics, can also be inclined onto bars, wallbars, bar boxes and used in a great variety of ways, producing not only two surfaces, narrow and wide, but creating space above and below.

Apparatus should be combined in many different ways and should be arranged appropriately to help children fulfil the tasks and challenges set.

## Tasks on Apparatus

When the work is new the whole class will need to be given the same task. For example if the challenge is to discover various ways of using hands and feet to travel, with the apparatus shared amongst six children the tasks might be as follows:

**Apparatus**—one form, two mats.

*Task* 1.—Experiment with a variety of ways in which the hands may be placed on the form, *e.g.* gripping the sides, placed on the form symmetrically, one on the form and the other on the floor, using hands alternately, placing the hands far apart or one in front of the other.

*Task* 2.—Explore the various take-offs and landings, which will include the five basic jumps.

*Task* 3.—Combine use of hands and feet, *e.g.* hands placed near each other on the form, feet kept astride the form, or using alternate hands to bear weight, keeping the feet together and making them go from side to side.

Once new apparatus is introduced, time should be given to enable the group to work freely exploring heights, surfaces, approaches, and landing points.

Having established six groups working on different arrangements of apparatus, tasks need to be set. Gradually as new movement ideas are introduced these tasks may vary, with half the class working on the new theme while the remainder have tasks related to work covered in the past. A class having worked on speeds and varying direction and level, for example, may begin to consider flight. Out of six pieces

C

of apparatus, three could be related to the new experience while the other groups work on time changes, level and direction. When partner work is begun after perhaps half a term, then the apparatus could change and tasks also. Three groups could now work on various aspects of partner work, while the teacher may decide to retain two sets of apparatus concerned with flight and the one remaining group may have a choice of task, stressing time changes, level or direction.

With groups of experienced third or fourth years the whole class could work on one particular theme, but explore different aspects, e.g. the class has worked on speed changes in an elementary way and used time variations on apparatus. Groups could now begin to experiment with the more advanced aspects, climaxes, accents, repetitive rhythms, time changes within a single action. Therefore six simple pieces of apparatus could be provided to cater for the various aspects of the one idea—see Chapter 7.

## CALMING DOWN

Just as the children need to be prepared bodily and mentally at the beginning of a lesson, so at the conclusion it is equally important to bring them together in order that they may recover from the excitement and stimulation of work on apparatus.

Slow, controlled movements should be suggested by the teacher, perhaps linked with symmetry or stretching and curling. If tasks are given which involve lowering parts of the body or balancing and returning to the normal standing position, points concerning poise and posture can be mentioned. Generally movements should be selected where the body moves as a whole, maintaining equilibrium and continuous contact with the floor.

This brief unwinding period at the end of a lesson enables the teacher to draw the class together, so that the session ends with the children as a unit rather than dispersing in small groups. It also means that as soon as one group has finished replacing apparatus, time need not be wasted waiting for others. The class can be trained to begin the calming activities in any space available, individuals eventually selecting their own movements.

CHAPTER 2

# MOVEMENT OBSERVATION

MOVEMENT is transient and in the teaching situation is rarely recorded by notation or by the camera. Therefore one way in which teachers and children widen their knowledge of movement is by trying to see and understand what is happening while it is happening. This is movement observation, the degree or depth of which will vary with the circumstances. Observation could be defined as seeing with understanding. In observing there is an active seeing of movement involving sympathetic participation by the observer rather than watching passively, or merely looking.

## OBSERVATION BY THE TEACHER

It is vital for a teacher to observe children, whatever the subject or situation. It is through observation that the successful teacher assesses the moods, attributes, needs and potential of individuals and groups. The observation of children moving should not be confined to the gymnastics lesson. Observing children at play, as they move around the school, in the classroom, as well as during other physical education activities, can be most valuable. In such situations the experienced observer can learn much about the children he is teaching through an understanding of their movement characteristics.

The Junior school teacher has a unique opportunity to know his pupils since he is with them in most of their daily activities. In the selecting of gymnastic material this knowledge should undoubtedly help him to widen their movement experience and cater for their movement needs. Conversely, what the Junior school teacher observes in the gymnastic lesson should be of value in the classroom, contributing to an all-round understanding of each child.

The physical education specialist in a Secondary school has the opportunity to become an expert observer of movement. However, he must realise that he is seeing children in one situation only, revealing though that situation undoubtedly is.

Although observation was used in the teaching of formal gymnastics, the process was made easy because the class usually worked at the same movement, at the same time. This meant that, in mass observation, those children who did not conform were easily distinguished. In addition, the faults in any one exercise could be anticipated and looked for.

21

In the teaching of gymnastics today it is essential that the teacher should observe well. Within a lesson the movement experience is guided by a series of tasks, each dependent upon the reaction to the preceding challenge. This demands acute observation. The difficulty arises because there are many answers to any given challenge and generally the teacher will have as many different solutions offered as there are children in the class. Moreover, there are no predetermined or fixed progressions. Unless the teacher is able to observe adequately it is unlikely that either he or his class will gain satisfaction from working in this manner, because of his inability to select, use and develop what he sees.

The ways in which a teacher observes his class generally are obvious and need only be mentioned. Juniors coming from a crowded classroom to the relative freedom of the hall or playground may immediately show a desire to exploit the space. Seeing this the teacher might give action tasks, such as running and jumping before expecting more controlled work as in balancing. Prior to the gymnastic lesson the Secondary class may have had a period where concentrated mental effort has been demanded. When the children are beginning to warm up, their movement sense may be dulled and their actions appear lethargic. Through a quick assessment of their mood the teacher may decide to prolong the limbering part of the lesson and devote time to a guided enlivening of the body.

General observation continues throughout the lesson and is the means by which the teacher can determine the achievements and understanding of the class as well as noting possible movement progressions.

At the same time the teacher is also concerned with more specific and immediate problems to which observation can provide the key to the answer. Once the class is challenged it is vital to see if the movement ideas involved have been understood and are being used profitably. As a result of his observation the teacher may need to clarify the task for the whole class, or it may be that individuals require further help.

Often the teacher may be looking for those whose response to a challenge is worth showing to the rest of the class. The way in which children can be helped to observe is dealt with later, but here the connection between observation by the teacher, selecting and "showing" is seen. In his selection the teacher is often setting a standard of work, therefore he should choose children whose work contains something of value. Demonstration in its narrowest sense (that this is the only way to answer the problem) is not a part of gymnastics. However, it is often expedient to select children to show their work to the rest of the class. It may be that several children are chosen because between them they have variety, or that they all have a particular point in common that the teacher wants to stress. Perhaps two or three will choose the same movement, *e.g.* balancing on hands, but each arranges the rest of his body differently and the teacher may wish to point out such possibilities to the rest of the class.

Selection by the teacher necessitates quick observation and this must be trained consciously. The poor observer may find himself faced with exciting activity from which he is unable to extract anything of significance. A pitfall to be avoided is that of looking only at those individuals who can be expected to find a worthwhile solution. Sometimes the same children show their work lesson after lesson, while the less spectacular or less able individuals are precluded even though they could make a valuable contribution. The skilled observer should be able to watch and select from the whole class.

Although of necessity much of the observation is concerned with the class or groups, opportunities should be taken to observe individuals. Through observation over a period of time the teacher can build up a valuable "movement picture" of each child. He can learn to recognise and help not only the skilled and the able but the lazy children, the foolhardy, the accident-prone, the nervous and those lacking confidence.

To the beginner it may appear as if this method of teaching is only for the expert observer of movement, but this is not so. All teachers are continuously adapting and adjusting their teaching material to the needs and reactions of their classes and this is often achieved by unconscious observation. However, it is stressed that to be successful in this work it is essential to observe movement consciously and to set out deliberately to train the faculty.

## Principles for Observing Gymnastics

In order to observe movement profitably it is necessary to have at least a basic knowledge of the principles of movement as formulated by Laban.* In the teaching of gymnastics the understanding of movement and movement observation are complementary; each will gain from the other.

When beginning to observe, the teacher may see only those aspects of movement to which he himself is sympathetic and stresses in his own work. However, just as the successful teacher avoids imposing his own movement preferences on his class, so the sympathetic observer must train himself to look for all aspects of gymnastics and not be confined by his own movement experiences.

The following is suggested as a framework upon which the teacher can build his observation of class and individual. Although it is

* For a detailed analysis concerned with all forms of movement see *The Mastery of Movement* by Rudolf Laban, 2nd edition revised by Lisa Ullmann.

hoped that teachers will endeavour to observe children moving in many situations, it is recognised that most observation of necessity takes place during a lesson. The headings are basic, being valid for both detailed and general observation. The examples given are not specific but are typical gymnastic situations that a teacher might observe.

In the observation of gymnastics the teacher's attention is upon four separate but related aspects.

1. *Body.*—The observer determines *what* the body is doing by looking at part, parts and the whole.
2. *Space.*—The observer sees *where* the body is moving by noting levels, directions and pathways.
3. *Speed and Energy.*—The observer considers *how* the body is moving by assessing the speed and the energy expended.
4. *Relationships* (with or without contact).—The observer notes the relation between the body and the floor, apparatus, partner and group, whilst movement is taking place.

## 1. BODY

In gymnastics many different actions can be distinguished. Some of these involve the body as a whole, while in others a part or parts are more important than the rest. It is the interplay and relation of parts to each other and to the whole body that concerns the observer.

Curling, stretching, twisting and jumping are examples of actions normally involving the whole body. Through observation the teacher determines if this is so or if parts are omitted from the action. In curling, the head is often neglected as well as sections of the spine. When stretching, children find difficulty in feeling this action through to their extremities, and so what is happening to the hands, head and feet needs to be observed. In flight children invariably anticipate the landing through lack of confidence. This results in the upper half of the body spoiling the flight, for instead of carrying on the upward thrust of the legs, the stress is downward, the focus being on the landing area. The teacher who observes these "bodily happenings" can then help his class to be more aware of what the body is doing and this should lead to more sensitive work.

In many actions, although the whole body is alive to the movement taking place, some parts by nature of their function have more emphasis than others. When sliding on the trunk occurs, the part of the body in contact with the ground is held in position, while one or more of the limbs provides propulsion by vigorous pushing or pulling. In such situations the limbs carry the main stress of the action. When a balance is held and then the weight transferred, the part that is to bear the weight assumes importance as it is prepared and placed in position.

In observing what the body is doing the teacher can see the extent to which the class needs further help. Similarly the next step in teaching can be determined. Suppose the task "experiment with balancing the body on asymmetric or uneven bases" is given. In this challenge what the body is doing is being stressed and the teacher would find his teaching points by observation along these lines:

1. Are all the ways of producing an uneven base being used—*i.e.* two unlike parts from different sides, or two parts from the same side, or two like parts placed unevenly?
2. Are individuals challenging themselves to the full, trying difficult inverted balances?
3. Are the balances being held or moved through?
4. Is there an awareness of what the rest of the body is doing above the base?

Whenever the challenges are related to body management or action tasks are given, the teacher should always observe the body first, for this ensures that the teaching point is pursued and developed. Often there is a temptation to deviate. An inexperienced teacher might follow the preceding task with the suggestion that the class "add variations of speed." This shows not only a lack of movement understanding but also poor observation. Progressions are based on the response to each challenge and it is unlikely that a class concerned with experimental balances will indicate a need to consider speed changes as well.

When observing the body, in addition to looking for the interplay between the parts and the whole, as in climbing a rope, the teacher must take other considerations into account. Sometimes the lower half is more important than the upper, as in taking off from the ground. Often one side is stressed more than the other, as in the beginning of a cartwheel. The movement possibilities of the body are virtually limitless, and persistent observation is required to recognise what is happening and then to act upon what is seen.

### 2. SPACE

The observation of the body in space during floorwork depends upon the task set. The spatial aspect may be of primary or secondary importance.

In a limbering task of "alternately travelling high in the air and low on the ground" the first observation would be directed towards the use of level. It would be necessary to see if the high and low levels were being exploited or if the movement was taking place in a meagre extension of the medium level. In a limbering task of "travelling on different body parts" it would be essential to ensure that this was happening before observing the use of directions. Levels, directions, pathways and body shape are often incidental to the main action of the body during floor work. Just as observation should not be directed immediately towards these aspects, so the class should not consider them until clarity and understanding of what the body is doing are shown.

Once a spatial theme is taken there is much to observe. In the task of "travel, using different directions" the observant teacher will see many variations. Some children will remain on an habitual pathway, such as circling the hall or gymnasium and while on this track will travel forwards, backwards or sideways. Others will concentrate on a varying track composed of lines, zig-zags, loops and curves which changes their front in relation to the space, but they retain one direction, usually forwards. Having realised this the teacher might re-word his challenge or decide to bring the different responses to the attention of the children by selecting a group for them to observe.

In advanced work the apparatus is often arranged so that each individual can select his own actions and pathways and here the teacher can observe if these are well correlated. One child might always approach each piece along a straight pathway, another only change direction on the floor between apparatus. A third might adjust and shift about on apparatus in order to change direction because of an inappropriate choice of action. Such situations may lead to difficulties and having observed the reasons for these the teacher should be able to offer constructive help.

### 3. Speed and Energy

Although what the body is doing is often of prime importance, how the body acts is also a vital consideration. When the speed of an action is assessed it is not sufficient to decide if the rate is quick or slow, although this is a beginning. Phases where acceleration or deceleration occur, as well as the rhythm and climax in a sequence, must be noted. A child may not get on to a high box because he has failed to build up his speed during his approach. Another child may be unable to hold a balance on a bar because he has not appreciated the need to decelerate into the balance. Actions such as jumping for a rope, helping a partner to achieve flight, landing on a narrow surface from a swing on a rope, are often inefficient because the timing is poor. A teacher who can appreciate when lack of timing defeats the aim of an action will have taken the first step towards being able to give positive help to his class.

When the output of energy is observed the use to which it is put is important. Many Secondary children, particularly girls, fail to get over high apparatus with weight on hands. This is because they cannot produce a strong pushing action in the upper part of the body or they do not realise that any change in tension is required. A teacher who by observation can pinpoint the reasons for inefficient and unsuccessful actions is more likely to help the performers than one whose comments remain at the "try harder," "get over next time" level.

Sometimes the speed and energy may appear secondary to what the body is doing. When attempting to roll for the first time, young Juniors will be best helped if attention is drawn to the action of the body rather than the speed and energy required. On acquiring the skill, however, it may be of great importance to stress these, particularly when the roll is one of a series or part of a sequence.

In many actions there is an equal stress on what the body is doing and how it performs the action. The take-off to achieve flight from the ground is a typical example. The action of the lower half is flexion into extension but unless this is done quickly and with considerable energy no flight results. In observing ineffective take-offs the teacher must see which of these vital ingredients is missing or over-stressed and help accordingly.

## 4. RELATIONSHIPS

In gymnastics the body can never finally be considered in isolation. Whatever the action there is always a relation between the body and the ground or apparatus or other people. This relation, whether it results in contact or not, is often taken for granted. A class showing little sensitivity usually reflects a teacher who has failed to observe well and consequently has done nothing to remedy the deficiency.

In getting on to a stage block from the floor with weight on hands a young Junior may not appreciate the importance of where he places his hands. He may put them too near the edge, so that there is little room for the rest of his body, or too far away, so that he is unable to take weight on them. Having observed this the teacher could suggest that he climbs on to the stage block and finds out where to place hands and feet in relation to each other.

The Secondary boy trying to swing from a rope to land on a box top some distance away will often continue to push the box from him not realising what is the cause. The teacher who has observed that the boy's approach is from the side instead of from above the box, or that the body is rigid instead of "waving up" over the feet on contact, is likely to help the boy be successful.

A Secondary girl attempting to roll along the top of a box might do this as if on a mat and consequently roll off the end. The teacher who observes that the girl is unaware of the relation between the length of her back, the size of her roll and the space available will probably be able to give constructive help.

In many activities which involve flight over apparatus, the placing of the hands determines what the rest of the body can do. When helping an individual in this situation, the teacher should observe where the hands are placed on the apparatus and how the rest of the body is used in relation to the hands, as this often indicates the rea- son for an unsuccessful attempt.

It is mentioned in the chapters devoted to partner and group work that such situations should not be explored until the teacher considers the class capable of benefiting from them. The decision to start such work will be based on knowledge of the class which has been built up by constant observation. Once working with others is taking place the teacher needs to be particularly alert to see that this is progressing in a safe and profitable way. Concern for the partner or group has to be encouraged and stimulated by the teacher.

When observing a small group trying out ways of lifting and lower- ing each other the teacher may be surprised by the amount of give and take that is necessary. He will see those who readily adapt to being one of a group and those who find this difficult. From his know- ledge of the individuals concerned the teacher will know the best way to deal with the situation observed, no two such occurrences ever being alike.

Having selected and presented a challenge to his class the teacher will normally know which aspect to observe first, whether "what" the body is doing is more important than "how" it is acting, and what to look for subsequently. However, it is often necessary to consider the movement as a whole to determine its main characteristics. This happens when a teacher finds that a child has decided what he wants to do in answer to a movement challenge but for some reason is un- able to carry out his intention. If the teacher is to help within the context of the situation he must observe what the child is trying to do and how he is setting about it, or, if this is not clear, ask for a verbal explanation.

The teacher must decide from his observation and knowledge of movement what are the essential characteristics of the action or series of actions, the inherent factors that make it what it is. For example, in jumping the body is always thrust into the air and although the jumps may vary in size the thrust is always present to a greater or lesser degree. Once these are determined they must be seen in relation to the child and how his attempt differs from that which will bring success. When these movement discrepancies have been discovered the teacher is in a position to give positive help.

It is through an understanding of movement, a knowledge of each child and observation that a teacher should be able to reconcile the movement essentials of actions with the ability and movement characteristics of the individual.

## OBSERVATION BY THE CLASS

Just as observation is vital to the teacher so children can be trained to observe and helped to profit from what they see. The visual is important as a way of learning and can help to widen an individual's movement vocabulary. Points which would otherwise remain obscure become clarified when watching classmates tackling a common problem. It is in seeing the variety of ways in which a challenge can be met that the scope of one movement idea is appreciated. This is particularly so when observation is followed immediately by the children trying out for themselves.

Young Juniors and beginners usually try to copy the actions seen. Later, children can select from the movement ideas observed and make them their own by modification and adjustment. The movement imagination is usually stimulated and enlivened by observation.

Secondly, through observation children begin to appreciate their own movement characteristics in relation to those of others. The child who naturally moves quickly can, by observation, recognise slow, deliberate movements. With the teacher's help this can be developed into an awareness of moving slowly when work is resumed. The ability to perceive one's own preferences as well as limitations can be encouraged by observation.

When beginning observation with a class the teacher has the alternatives of:

1. Selecting two or three individuals whose work is worth showing to the rest of the class; or
2. Dividing the class in half so that each group in turn observes and moves.

In the former, the observation is made easy but the children showing may be self-conscious. In the latter, the observation is difficult but those moving are unlikely to be inhibited, and each child experiences both situations. Whichever method is used the teacher has two groups both of which need guidance in order to benefit from the experience.

*The observers* should be given one point to look for first, *e.g.*

"What parts of the body take weight?"
"Is there an increase or decrease in speed?"
"Which direction is being stressed?"

As skill in observing increases more than one movement aspect can be considered, *e.g.*

"What is the essential difference between these two sequences?"
"What have these people in common?"
"What varying relationships occur in this group sequence?"

After observation the children should be able to make a quick analysis of what they have seen and offer constructive criticism.

*The performers* may need to be told beforehand that their work is to be seen. This ensures that they are prepared both mentally and physically. Some children naturally enjoy being selected and this often provides motivation for further effort. Others lack confidence but the teacher can do much to create an atmosphere of mutual help so that this difficulty is eventually overcome. Having shown his work the mover should receive helpful comments. Occasionally sequences may be selected that only partially fulfil a challenge. This situation must be handled carefully by the teacher. It can be successful only when the relationships are such that the performers have confidence in the sympathy and understanding of the teacher and the rest of the class. Then an exchange of ideas and views can be valuable and do much to add to the appreciation of the movement principles involved.

Another way for children to observe is by dividing the class into couples, each child observing his partner in turn. This method has advantages in that the observation is directed towards one person and the performer is unlikely to be self-conscious. It is essential in this situation that the teacher gives specific observation points. The disadvantages are that some of the work seen will not be particularly good and the teacher cannot easily check that all the couples have profited by the experience.

After observation, it is essential that the class works again at the same task. The children who observed must be given a chance to put what they have seen and learnt into practice. Those who performed will have been given help which they can now implement. When the whole class resumes work it is an excellent opportunity for the teacher to see if the time spent on observation has been worth while.

The teacher should be able to use class observation appropriately. In starting a new gymnastic theme observation is of little value when the work is at the early exploratory stage. Too much observation too soon can be limiting. In partner and group work observation naturally happens during the working out of ideas. This not only enables movements to be matched where applicable but also fosters sympathetic work.

The development of sequences takes time, and experience is needed in selection. Observation is one way in which appreciation of logical movement can be gained. Children are invariably able to see this first in the work of others before they can make a similar assessment of their own efforts.

In observation, children are given the opportunity not only of watching others but also of adding to their movement understanding. Through their observation they should be led towards an appreciation of movement which is relevant to the challenge. They should be aware that a movement is pleasing and should understand what makes it so. Children can appreciate good movement without detailed knowledge of what it entails.

The place of observation in any one lesson needs careful consideration. Abused it can kill the pace of a lesson, used skilfully it enhances both movement and understanding. Young children and beginners do not need to observe often but, with training, children can profit by short intensive sessions. The experienced teacher will probably include observation by the class of floor or apparatus work or both in most lessons. It is through an understanding of the value of this way of working, and seeing it in relation to teaching gymnastics generally that a teacher is most likely to use observation profitably.

# CHAPTER 3

# ELEMENTARY BODY MANAGEMENT

THE ability to control and manage the body would appear as one of the main essentials in any given movement situation. In gymnastics this is certainly a prior consideration. Children must first be guided towards an awareness of the capabilities of the body. Later they can be helped to acquire the mastery needed, in terms of control and management, to gain enjoyment and satisfaction from objective work, and to exploit the movement potential of the body to the full.

Unlike learning a foreign language, gymnastic movement is not new to the beginner; children, however young, will have already gained a degree of bodily skill, and will certainly have experienced joy and satisfaction in moving. Once the child is placed in the learning situation, however, although use is made of movements he has already mastered, the emphasis now is on awakening a conscious knowing of what the body is doing, of how it is moving, and where it is going. Once this awareness has been fostered, the children's habitual movements are extended to include new skills, which when mastered, become part of a wider, more varied movement vocabulary.

The term "body awareness" has become an overworked one in recent years but in this text the phrase is intended to cover the re-awakening of the kinesthetic sense. In everyday life it is essential that each individual evolves a basic vocabulary of habit actions, such as walking, sitting, eating and dressing. Although the kinesthetic sense has been involved in the acquisition of these skills, conscious effort in performing them lessens until eventually they become habitual and a conscious awareness of what is happening is no longer required. In civilised communities, interest in and awareness of movement are on the whole subdued; movements tend to be restricted and restrained, children's actions become inhibited and retarded through contact with a variety of circumstances. It is this awareness of what the body is doing, how one part moving affects the whole, and the relation and interplay of body parts in action, which must be stimulated if the movement vocabulary and ability of individuals is to become enriched and vital.

The following elementary movement ideas of Locomotion, Stillness, Weight Bearing and Transference of Weight all involve guiding children towards an awareness of the body. Although there is variety within this selection a certain correlation exists but for clarification each aspect is considered in isolation. It should be noted that these are dealt with in a form of progression so that each new idea utilises the knowledge and skill acquired in previous work.

## LOCOMOTION

### *Material*

Locomotion, that is travelling, is achieved by the transference of weight from one part of the body either to the same part, or to another in succession. This is normally brought about by weight being transferred on the feet, involving one or both, as in stepping, running, hopping or skipping, but in gymnastics this is by no means the only method. Ground can be covered by hands supporting the weight of the body while feet travel, overtaking or following, as in cartwheels and crouch jumps. Another way of travelling where contact with the floor is maintained is when the body is kept curled and compact as in rolling, which can be experienced on a variety of body surfaces and in any direction. When the body is ejected into the air and flight takes place, the body travels through space, and although this too is usually achieved from feet to feet, other parts can be used to eject and receive body weight, and it is possible to bounce on parts such as hips, shins and hands. The body can be moved from one place to another in a sliding action, which usually involves large surfaces such as front, back or hips. In this instance although travelling results, the body itself may or may not move, for after the initial impetus the shape can change or the position be maintained whilst sliding takes place.

### *Teaching*

Although locomotion is a fundamental aspect of gymnastics, in the early stages of introducing this work to children, it is dealt with in a very elementary way. It is perhaps the best starting point, as most young children are interested in ways of getting from one place to another, and are concerned with the "going" and with the parts of the body used when covering ground.

It is sufficient at this stage to experiment with the body in order to discover the variety possible within travelling, and experience should be given in the number of ways in which feet or hands and feet are used in conjunction. Children should be encouraged to use the trunk as well as parts of the limbs on which to progress and resulting actions should include such activities as crawling, shuffling, sliding, running, hopping, leaping, rolling and rocking. (*See* Plate 1.)

Young children should not be expected to link actions as they are often unable to change readily from one to another. Juniors and first year Secondary children enjoy repeating the same action several times and can be encouraged to do this. In some cases a rhythm will be established in repetition which children find most exciting and satisfying. Action sequences including various ways of travelling can be introduced at this stage where simple transitions only are involved and weight bearing is restricted to a limited number of body parts. These can be related to the natural reactions of children to certain situations, e.g. Juniors most naturally run, jump, land and slide to a stop; or run, jump and turn in the air, land and roll; whilst to run, dive and slide would be a logical action sequence for most boys.

A later development for older children is to combine travelling actions where they learn to move easily and with agility throughout a sequence with a number of body parts taking weight in turn.

Teaching points concerned with receiving and transferring weight are dealt with later in this Chapter.

*Apparatus*

The elementary aspect of locomotion will mainly concern Junior teachers; however the specialist teaching the first year in the Secondary school may be faced with tackling the same theme, but will probably have a greater variety of apparatus with which to work. Suggestions for work on apparatus are, therefore, dealt with separately for Juniors, although the principles of providing apparatus for work on locomotion remain the same for any age group.

Opportunities should be given for travelling with specific body parts suggested—

1. on the feet,
2. using hands and feet,
3. on hands only,

or the stress can be on bodily actions—

4. by sliding,
5. by rolling,
6. by gripping and releasing alternately.

1. LOCOMOTION ON THE FEET

Obstacles should be provided to jump over, to get in and out of, or on and off, along, or to go from side to side.

*Juniors.*—Apparatus such as canes or hoops supported on skittles, individual mats, ropes and jumping stands, planks, chairs, low tables and steps all provide suitable challenges for this activity.

*Secondary.*—Forms used both narrow and broad side uppermost and slightly inclined, mats and mattresses, give sufficient opportunity for

PLATE 1.—Task: Travel keeping contact with the floor

PLATE 2.—Examples of apparatus where gripping can be explored

Plate 3

Plate 4

Plate 5

first years to experiment with the basic idea of travelling using feet only, but these can be supplemented by any of the above suggestions in the Junior section.

## 2. LOCOMOTION USING HANDS AND FEET

The class can be introduced to the idea that hands can lead while feet follow, that hands can lead and feet overtake, that hands and feet can be on the same or on different levels, and the limbs can work together or alternately.

*Juniors.*—Ladders or planks used horizontally or inclined on stools or climbing frames, ropes or nets where the children can clamber and scramble and climb, would be sufficient to enable them to travel producing a large variety of ideas.

*Secondary.*—Forms used as previously stated, Danish bars, Cave Southampton apparatus or any type of hinged wallbars, rope or wooden climbing ladders and box tops, will all give the beginners sufficient variety with which to experiment.

## 3. LOCOMOTION ON HANDS ONLY

As it is impossible for the majority of children to travel on the floor taking weight on hands alone, this possibility should be thoroughly explored on apparatus. There are two essential differences between using the hands on the floor and on apparatus. One is that on apparatus the hands are able to grip, an action impossible on a flat surface. Secondly, whereas on the floor the body must be above the hands if these are to support the weight, on apparatus it may be suspended below the weight bearing part, an entirely different experience. The hands may move alternately but not overtaking each other as in swinging sideways along a bar, or one may pass the other as when the body travels in the forward and backward direction. Hanging, swinging and climbing are all activities which will answer this task.

*Juniors.*—Rope or other types of ladder, balance bars and climbing frames provide the children with opportunities for exploring the above ideas.

*Secondary.*—Girls can experiment on bars at hanging height, travelling along and moving in all three directions, while some may also be able to travel up a rope or across a number of ropes taking weight on hands only. Boys will probably enjoy the challenge of swarming a rope or ladder using hands alone and will also produce a greater variety of methods of progressing along bars.

D

4. LOCOMOTION BY SLIDING

This activity can occur on raised surfaces, parallel or inclined to the ground. The body can be pulled along the top or underneath with a number of parts being used.

*Juniors.*—Balance bars or planks inclined on to stools or raised between two stools, slippery topped tables or forms offer situations for pulling up, sliding along or down a variety of surfaces.

*Secondary.*—This is not an activity that needs to be pursued at any length but it can be dealt with adequately using inclined forms at a variety of heights and bars at hip level to give first years an experience of what is involved in the action.

5. LOCOMOTION BY ROLLING

If this action is to be attempted with confidence on apparatus, then it must be preceded by sufficient practice at floor level. The apparatus at first should be comparatively low, broad and stable and the individual should be expected to complete the roll on the apparatus provided, *i.e.* arrive on the apparatus, roll and get off. The obvious progressions are dealt with in the section on transference of weight and in Chapter 10. Older Juniors and young Secondary classes could be expected, however, to manage quite a number of these.

*Juniors.*—Table tops, wide planks, forms and stage blocks, are surfaces that can be used, provided they are not too high and are safe in all respects.

*Secondary.*—Children should be given the opportunity of experimenting with a variety of rolls on surfaces such as forms and box tops, and the majority should be able quite quickly to progress to some of the more difficult ways of rolling on apparatus.

6. LOCOMOTION BY GRIPPING AND RELEASING ALTERNATELY

This has already been mentioned with reference to travelling using hands only. In addition to this, however, children can be helped to explore other parts of the body capable of gripping, which can often be used in conjunction with hands to produce locomotion. These parts such as the toes, instep, back of the knees and front of the hips cannot be included as weight bearing bases when travelling at floor level, but once on apparatus can, if necessary, support the whole weight of the body.

*Juniors.*—Any type of climbing frame, ropes or supported ladders and poles are suitable for children to experience the gripping action which is such a basic requirement for all work on apparatus (Plate 2).

*Secondary.*—Climbing frames, hinged wall bars, window ladders, bars, ropes, bar boxes and the horse pommels offer a variety of gripping situations.

In the early stages of planning apparatus for young Juniors, the teacher merely sets the scene, providing the situation which will lead the children quite naturally towards experiencing the greatest variety of activities possible. Provision should be made so that many of the above activities can be included, with each piece of apparatus dealing with a particular aspect of locomotion. Once the class begin to work on apparatus the teacher can help to widen the children's movement vocabulary by setting simple tasks that stimulate them to discover new ways of using the body when travelling. He must also ensure that each child is given the opportunity of working on several different pieces of apparatus and eventually tackling them all over a period of time.

With older Juniors and Secondary classes, apparatus can provide opportunities to include a variety of methods of travelling, *e.g.* gripping and sliding, sliding and rolling, jumping over and rolling, while they can also be encouraged to travel over the apparatus using many pathways, travelling in a straight line, making a circular or zig-zag track.

Plate 3 illustrates a class of 7-year-olds working on locomotion with a variety of apparatus.

## STILLNESS

### *Material*

The body travelling and the body in stillness must both be experienced if true awareness and management are to be appreciated. Although in the early stages of mastering stillness it will suffice that movement is checked and body weight controlled, it should be realised that stillness does not merely mean "to stop moving." It implies that movement is held so that the muscular tension involved in arresting an action and maintaining a still position can be experienced. This should be considered as an "active pause" rather than cessation of movement; a positive attitude should be adopted towards stillness in which appropriate tension is felt and used to maintain the position of the body.

Actions can be brought under control and stopped in several ways. If the body is kept compact and all angular parts brought within the curved shape, once the body is set in motion movement will be continuous until a time when the original momentum is lost. If, however, a flat part of the body is released, such as a forearm, and comes in contact with the floor, or the body itself is uncurled, movement will be interrupted. At that point, an abrupt stop can be achieved providing sufficient bodily tension can be produced to check the forward momentum at the moment when weight is received on the flat part.

An abrupt stop is not always necessary, however, and stillness can be brought about by a gradual loss of momentum. When a landing from a jump which involves tilting or turning takes place, there will be a momentary loss of control and inability to halt the action unless the distribution of body weight is adjusted correctly. One way of recovering equilibrium would be to continue to move, following the direction of body weight and to round the body so that weight can quickly be transferred from feet to other parts. This may result in a rolling action where the speed can be controlled once the feet come into contact with the ground and grip the surface, or it may lead into a rocking motion where momentum can slowly decrease, resulting in eventual stillness.

Speed can be checked and a running action brought to a stop by ejecting the body into the air. In order to achieve the upward thrust at take-off the forward lean of the body has to be altered. This opposing of the forward momentum by the vertical ejection is instrumental in initially checking the speed of the run. When considering the most effective way of stopping the action, it will be found that of the five basic jumps, the two to two is the most efficient. In a double take-off an initial interruption of speed occurs while one foot meets the other and the body is brought into symmetry. On landing on two feet the body is more likely to be controlled and stable and an immediate stop can be effected in two ways. Movement can be checked through space when, on landing, the body flexes and regains the normal position with the landing and recovery taking place on the same spot. Secondly, there can be a complete cessation of movement within the body itself when a gripping action on arrival holds the landing position. The first method of stopping is the more usual and natural bodily resilience should be encouraged. The second is occasionally resorted to in some emergency landings and also used in the more advanced aspects of balance.

However, the more usual method of take-off and landing is from one foot to two. In this instance the asymmetrical running action remains unaltered in the take-off and it will not be until the feet come together in the air that symmetry is achieved, but ultimately this does take place and preparation can then be made for a two foot landing, and as previously stated stillness may then result.

The stability and control achieved from a two foot landing obviously assists ultimate stillness. This may not be an immediate necessity and the performer may find it requires a following jump or number of resilient jumps in order to control fully the momentum gathered in the preparation and the actual leap itself. In this case speed can be lost gradually, the height and tension involved in the bounces following the landing will decrease steadily until full control is experienced and a stop is made possible.

Movement can be performed with either free or bound flow. Free flow is apparent in movements which are difficult to stop at any given point; bound flow is when the control is such that actions can easily be checked. It will be recognised that in gymnastics free flow is usually inappropriate, and that the attitude towards flow is one concerned mainly with actions which are sufficiently controlled to allow for quick adjustment, adaptation or immediate stillness. In dealing with stillness it should be realised that the body control involved in achieving this is of great importance when considering safety in any movement situation.

## *Teaching*

With young Juniors, mastering stillness will be a major step in managing body weight. Children have little inclination to stop actions, being mainly concerned with travelling; in some instances it is only due to the fact that they become exhausted that movement eventually ceases. In the early stages the teacher must be prepared to dictate the moment of stopping and yet not expect a common response. Very few will be able to bring about anything but a gradual cessation of movement. Another way of helping children to experience stopping is to give them situations where a natural stop occurs, as in sliding, swivelling and spinning. This could be developed by helping them to contrast feeling the gradual petering out of movement in these actions, with a deliberate stopping of a slide or a spin, and experiencing the held position. Later, individuals can evolve their own phrases of movement and although this is a difficult stage the teacher must be patient and persist, helping them to clarify the starting and final positions as well as paths followed and actions performed. The stillness achieved at this stage will consist merely of the movement petering out; there will be no feeling of completion or any anticipation of what is to follow; nor will the attention be directed towards the position of the body whilst immobile.

Once the initial stage of controlling the body has been mastered so that stillness results, children should be able to employ this ability in more difficult situations. They should become adept at avoiding obstacles and other children by stopping abruptly and be able to react to any situation requiring immediate stillness.

It is at this stage that weight bearing on different parts may be introduced. If this is attempted before children have been given sufficient time to become accustomed to the tension which has to be produced before stillness is achieved, the results will be disappointing and little satisfaction will be experienced. Stillness here will involve a deliberate interruption of the action and attention will be focused on the part or parts of the body bearing weight, rather than on the movements leading into and out of the arrival. There will probably be little or no feeling of the true balance or poise which will be developed when greater bodily skill has been mastered. The advanced technique involved in balance includes awareness of the manner in which the balance is achieved and lost.

### Apparatus

The teacher of younger children is concerned more with action than stillness on apparatus, but the ability to stop or change direction to avoid others or obstacles is something that children must eventually learn to include in managing the body.

They can be helped to master the skill of checking movement by first experiencing the control required when changing direction. This can be accomplished with each child working individually on small apparatus.

**Apparatus**—individual mats.
    *Task.*—Run and jump over the mat, turn and roll back.

**Apparatus**—a skipping rope on the floor.
    *Task.*—Jump from side to side using feet only, at the end turn and come back using hands and feet to travel.

**Apparatus**—skittles and cane.
    *Task.*—Run and jump over the cane, turn and slide back underneath.

Inclined planks can also help children to control the impetus of movement, *e.g.* when travelling up a steeply inclined surface using feet only or hands and feet, the speed naturally decelerates as the top is reached. As momentum is lost the action becomes more easily controlled and a pause is quite simply effected. Similarly, when sliding down, a stop at the bottom is the usual result.

Repetitive actions along forms, planks or benches can help the performer to appreciate phrasing, while the child chooses for himself how many times the action is to be repeated before stopping.

Older Juniors and lower Secondary classes can be expected to perform slightly more difficult tasks such as showing moments of stillness during a sequence on apparatus or experimenting with the task of finding different ways of arriving and holding a position on a given piece of apparatus. Wall bars, climbing frame, ropes, bars, box and horse can be used in the latter case.

Stillness should be seen as a contrast to locomotion and introduced in connection with travelling, but very soon the point at which the teacher can lead the class into weight bearing will become apparent.

## WEIGHT BEARING

### Material

Man's specialised way of using the body, that is, in the upright position, is not the main concern in gymnastics; the aim is to exploit the body to the full and to utilise the movement potential in as versatile a way as possible. Weight bearing suggests that the weight of the body is above the supporting part; therefore on the floor weight bearing means that the body is completely supported on a chosen base. Locomotion and stillness are both related to this new idea because while travelling weight has to be controlled and held over the supporting part.

Many parts of the body are capable of taking weight but it will be discovered that some lend themselves more readily to producing a steady, stable base than others. The placement of these parts in relation to the floor and the rest of the body is also important. It appears natural in the early stages of weight bearing to use flat parts or parts that can be flattened such as shoulders, shins, hips, forearm and hands and to place these symmetrically.

As well as weight being equally distributed over two body parts which are the same, two or more different parts may be used which produce an equally steady base, e.g. a shin and forearm, or a shin and two hands. The larger the base relative to the rest of the body, the steadier the position. It will be found when maintaining weight on two different parts that it is simpler to use right and left sides of the body. A progression will be to take weight on two different parts of the body using the same side, this requiring greater ability to control the body weight.

Later when greater skill has been acquired, the asymmetrical placing of parts can be exploited. Body weight can be held on a part of the trunk such as one hip or one shoulder, but a far more difficult challenge would be to produce an asymmetrical base using one or two limbs.

Rounded parts of the body can be used to support weight but when, for example, the head, knee or elbow forms the base other parts may be needed to stabilise the position.

While maintaining weight on one or more parts, the rest of the body may remain still or may move. In a cartwheel, for example, the body weight is supported on the hands, while the rest of the body, extended, wheels over the support. While bearing weight on the shoulders the body may be still or moving over the base while another part is prepared to receive the weight.

Weight may be received and maintained on parts of the body for a brief period or can be held for a comparatively long time, while the performer uses the freed parts. When taking weight either partially or wholly on the shoulders the legs may be symmetrical, reaching away from the ground, they may remain together or be far apart, one may bend and the other stretch, they may twist against the shoulders and circle, or one leg may reach out and the toe touch the floor whilst the other reaches up and away from the body. (*See* Plate 4.)

Weight bearing must be considered in relation to body awareness: in the first instance, the actual contact with the floor of different body parts heightens the kinesthetic sense; secondly, when weight is taken on parts not normally used, the rest of the body is placed in a completely new situation and learning to manage the body in this novel position presents a considerable physical challenge. When inverted, for example, reach and mobility alter and a complete re-orientation is necessary.

Finally, in the consideration of work on apparatus which requires negotiating different levels and using the body's full potential, awareness and ability to manage the body in any situation is seen to be invaluable.

## Teaching

The child, having explored methods of travelling and mastered the skill involved in checking an action, can now experiment with the idea that weight can be received on and supported by a number of different parts of the body. At first the teacher may need to help the class by suggesting that parts such as shoulders, hips and knees can bear the weight of the rest of the body. The children can then be encouraged to experiment for themselves, *e.g.* exploring the possibilities of weight bearing on all matching parts of the body, such as hands, forearms, shins. These activities will be performed first in isolation but once the children have mastered a few possibilities, they can then be expected to attempt to link travelling and stopping with reference to weight bearing. At this point the teacher may have to refer back to the ways of travelling previously experienced, if the children limit themselves to using hands and feet only.

In order to develop the idea that two identical parts can bear the body's weight, it could be suggested that hands, for example, can be placed near together, farther apart, side by side or one in front of the other.

The next progression is to encourage the use of dissimilar parts of the body forming an asymmetrical base, and the class will probably produce many possibilities with this idea in mind.

Older children could be presented with the task of discovering iso-lated parts of the body on which weight can safely be taken, *e.g.* one hip, one shin or one shoulder, or experimenting with the possibility of producing uneven bases which result in a tipping of the body, *e.g.* hand and forearm, knee and shoulder.

Movement habits are easily established at this stage and it is here that the teacher can help children to experiment equally with right and left sides of the body so that weight is received as often on one as on the other. Throughout this aspect of the work the teacher should emphasise that care must be taken in placing parts in order to receive weight and point out that these parts can often be prepared in the previous movement. Most children naturally prepare for action; this can be seen in the girls' preparatory forward swing of the arms and backward movement of the top half of the body before attempting a handstand, and in the attitude most boys adopt at the start of a race, or before a measured jump.

Once children have become aware of the possibilities of weight bearing and have experienced a fair proportion, they can begin to give some attention to the ways in which the rest of the body can be used while it is supported on any given base. Whilst weight is being borne on the hands, for example, the rest of the body can be elon-gated as in a handstand, it can be taken through a wide, stretched shape as in a cartwheel, it can be kept relatively compact as in a "Chinese" handstand, or crouch jump, or it can turn and twist in the air or move over the hands. These are only a few named skills and many others can be invented once the class grasp the principle. (*See* Plate 5.)

During the exploratory stages of this idea, the child will merely be resting on the weight bearing part. With older Juniors, and at an early stage with Secondary children, the teacher should make the point that the rest of the body produces the appropriate amount of tension, enabling the performer to feel that the body is held in posi-tion over the point of contact with the floor. This is to ensure that the child maintains a liveliness within the body, alert to any action which might follow. Just as children's carriage is noted when in the normal positions of standing and sitting, so too, when weight is taken on other parts of the body, rather than allowing a collapse or slump, the teacher should encourage readiness, anticipation and a feeling of poise.

Up to this point the attention of the class will have been directed towards the part or parts of the body providing the base and the ability of the freed parts to be held or move in a variety of ways. Once the child's attention becomes concerned with ways of arriving, as well as resulting actions, this leads naturally into consideration of methods of weight transference.

## Apparatus

When apparatus is introduced not only has a variety of surfaces and levels to be considered but new parts of the body can now take weight and different combinations of body parts can be used as supports.

### SINGLE APPARATUS

When providing apparatus situations for this theme it is advisable to allow children time to work on single pieces of apparatus before confronting them with combinations. It is also helpful in the early stages to have the whole class using similar apparatus, *e.g.* everyone working on forms, or mats or a combination of bars and mats. Introducing this idea simply ensures that each child builds a considerable repertoire of ways of using single pieces of apparatus. This will be found of value later when groups are expected to work on a combination or circuit where forms, mats and bars are used in conjunction with larger apparatus.

**Apparatus**—mats.
> *Task 1.*—Cross taking weight on the hands, return with weight on another part.
> *Task 2.*—Approach with weight taken alternately on hands and feet, cross using parts of the trunk.

**Apparatus**—forms.
> *Task 1.*—Travel along the form with weight on hands, feet going from side to side.
> *Task 2.*—Using one part of the body on the form and another on the floor, travel from end to end.

**Apparatus**—bars (hanging height).
> *Task 1.*—Experiment with ways of getting from one end to the other using hands or feet or both.
> *Task 2.*—Experiment with hanging positions where weight bearing parts are the highest.

**Apparatus**—window ladders.
> *Task 1.*—Travel up or across using hands and feet alternately.
> *Task 2.*—Travel up or across using hands and a part of the body other than feet.

**Apparatus**—a low box.
> *Task 1.*—Get from one side to the other with one part only touching the apparatus, approach from any angle.
> *Task 2.*—Arrive on feet and get off.

COMBINATIONS OF APPARATUS

The following are examples of combinations of apparatus which offer varying levels.

**Apparatus**—two ropes and a mattress.

*Task* 1.—Using one or two ropes, jump up on to the apparatus, feet to be lowered gradually. On contact with the floor transfer the weight on to other parts of the body such as knees, hips or shoulders.

*Task* 2.—Preparation as in previous task but instead of lowering so that feet touch first, other parts of the body make first contact with the floor.

**Apparatus**—bar (medium height), low box, mat.

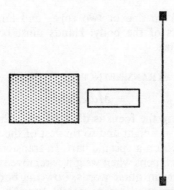

*Task*.—Hands must be used to lead the body from one piece of apparatus to the other, therefore they must be the first part of the body to contact each new piece of apparatus.

**Apparatus**—bar (hip height), saddle, bar box, mat.

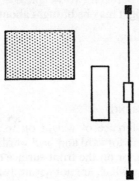

*Task.*—A different part of the body must make first contact with each piece of apparatus.

**Apparatus**—ropes, low box, two mats.

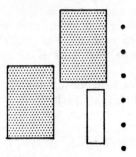

*Task.*—Swing from one or two ropes and land on the box on different parts of the body. Hands must be the first part to touch the mats.

## TRANSFERENCE OF WEIGHT

### *Material*

In weight bearing the focus is directed towards the part or parts which are to receive weight and to the rest of the body while weight is being maintained on a specific part. In transference of weight the stress is on what happens when weight is removed from one part and arrives on another; in other words, how the body moves between two points of support. Whereas weight bearing is concerned with stillness, transference of weight involves locomotion. Although there is a correlation between transference of weight and locomotion, the emphasis is different. In locomotion it is on the travelling, getting from place to place, while in transference of weight it is on the movement which lies between two weight bearing positions.

Transference of weight may be brought about by any of four ways:

1. rocking and rolling,
2. sliding,
3. step-like actions,
4. flight.

### 1. ROCKING AND ROLLING

This involves transference of weight on to adjacent body parts, *i.e.* along the spine as in forward and backward rolls, across the back as in sideways rolling, or on the front surface of the trunk. In some cases parts of the body which are not naturally adjacent can be made so. The feet can be brought near to the hips in a crouch position so that a movement where weight is transferred down the spine can be taken, without interruption, on to the heel and then the ball of the foot. The curved surface is maintained, allowing the rocking or rolling action already established to continue.

Rocking differs slightly from rolling in that in rocking the weight is transferred on to adjacent parts and is brought back again along the same line of supports in reverse. In rolling the weight is transferred once along the spine and then eventually taken on to another body part. Rocking leads very naturally into rolling and vice versa.

## 2. SLIDING

Sliding is another method whereby the body weight is transferred from one place to another while in constant contact with the supporting surface, but where it is not always true to say that weight has been transferred from one part to another. When children slide it is usually as a result of a run and dive, and in this instance the weight of the body is maintained on the same area, hips, side or front, while the body is carried along the ground. The initial impetus comes from the speed generated in the run and dive on to the floor and locomotion will continue until this energy is spent.

When the body is sliding on a comparatively large area other parts may be used to provide added propulsion but it is only incidental that they bear part of the weight of the body. In a sliding action on the hips the heels may be used intermittently to push and so maintain the original slide. While taking weight on the front surface of the body the hands, used alternately or together, can pull or push the body along the floor and thereby assist the slide.

## 3. STEP-LIKE ACTIONS

Step-like transferences of weight resemble the process used in walking. In considering the walking action it can be seen that from standing on two feet, weight is shifted on to one whilst the other is lifted, prepared and placed in a new position. As weight is transferred on to the new support there is a moment when weight is equally distributed over the two feet, before being taken on to the foot last grounded and the process repeated, each foot overtaking the other in turn. Step-like transferences of weight can take place using a number of body parts, and in actions such as handstands and cartwheels this is the type of weight transference used, hands and feet alternately acting as supports for the rest of the body.

## 4. FLIGHT

In the three methods of transferring weight mentioned previously, contact with the floor has been maintained. In the fourth method, momentary loss of contact with the ground is experienced and flight is achieved.

Transference of weight by means of flight is usually made from feet to feet or feet to hands, but flight can be gained by using other parts of the body. In bouncing activities flight is achieved from, and weight received on to, the same body part. Hands and feet can be used alternately with flight taking place between the push off from the feet and the landing on the hands or vice versa. This will be only momentary flight but the period in the air will be prolonged with the more skilful performer. Resilient landings, where the ability of the body to rebound is exploited, will be encouraged in bouncing and continuous leaping, while landing from a height and at speed may necessitate weight being transferred quickly on to another part. Use can be made here of the three other methods of weight transference.

Effective ejection, use of the body in the air and safety on landing are discussed in Chapter 12.

## Teaching

Although transference of weight is a fundamental gymnastic theme, it will depend upon the age and movement preference of the class where the teacher begins. With a class of Juniors who are lively and energetic the starting point could be with flight and sliding, whereas when older Secondary girls are being introduced to this type of work, the teacher would be well advised to begin with step-like transferences. Wherever the start is made, all four ways should be introduced, following reasonably quickly upon each other.

Flight and step-like actions involve the body in changing situations, whereas once the body assumes the curled shape and begins rolling, no change occurs until the action alters. The bodily situation remains comparatively unchanged in sliding also, once the action is begun. In teaching transference of weight therefore, it is as well to cover two methods in one lesson if a balance of activity is to be achieved, *e.g.* rolling and step-like actions could be taken together or activities which include flight and sliding could be combined.

### 1. ROCKING AND ROLLING

Rocking on parts of the body suited to this activity is a good preparation for rolling as the appropriate surfaces will be discovered and the necessity for rounding these areas will be appreciated. When rocking on the back it can be pointed out that slight rocking can be produced when only a small area of the back is used, or a more vigorous action is possible if the weight is transferred along the complete line of the spine. If the feet are tucked in and made to produce a continuation of line with the back and hips, the rock can extend to the heel and ball of the foot and the movement can then continue in reverse. Children can experience rocking not only on to two feet placed side by side, but also on to two feet with one placed in front of the other. This not only extends the rocking action slightly but is useful later in gaining continuity of action in recovery. If, for example, having completed a rocking action which is to be followed by a cartwheel or a handstand, the feet are placed one in front of the other, this will lead the body more smoothly into these actions than if weight were equally distributed over the two.

One activity for children to practise is rocking forwards and backwards on the back, gradually gaining momentum, including the feet in the action, and when sufficient energy and speed have been gathered, transferring weight on to feet, either allowing the body to continue in the forward direction or ejecting the body into the air. Having introduced the possibility that weight can be transferred on to feet at the completion of a rocking action, the child can now experiment with the idea that as the feet or the shoulders receive weight, the rest of the body is free to be redirected by a slight twist of the top or lower half against the fixed part.

Children should experience both the convexity and concavity of the spine and having discovered the possibilities of rocking on the back, the front surface of the body should be used. Some will find rocking along the front of the body, transferring the weight from the chest to the hips, quite difficult as this requires considerable strength and mobility. Once they have felt the two extremes of curling and arching the spine, some children will find this useful on apparatus. The active use of the upper and lower half of the body in this method of rocking should be encouraged and ways of leading into and twisting out of this action can be discovered.

A rocking action can also be effected by using the back from right to left of the spine, resulting in a side to side movement. The body, in this case, can be elongated or curled. The arms should be tucked in and the front of the body contracted so that the shoulders and back are rounded as much as possible, allowing maximum rocking to take place across the whole area. Once this has been mastered, ways of getting into and out of this position by transferring weight on to parts such as knees, forearms and hands which present themselves naturally when completing this type of rock, can be explored.

Within rocking, the speed changes and the pauses which occur before a change of direction give the child a valuable experience. He can learn to increase and decrease momentum and discover the resulting rhythms, whilst the hesitation felt as the rocking action reaches the end of its path is perhaps a new experience for most. It is when performing such actions that children begin to appreciate the inherent time stresses. It can also provide them with background knowledge which can be used to advantage at a later stage when changes of speed within actions are considered. With younger classes and to some extent with older children, this may not be so—it may not involve them in a conscious awareness—but if the teacher understands and gives the children the bodily experience, this is sufficient until such time as they become capable of coping intellectually.

Although most children will have rolled quite naturally before, they will not have experienced all the possibilities, their preference probably being towards asymmetrical actions. As a safety precaution the teacher needs to stress that in rolling the body as a whole must be curled, presenting a rounded surface to the floor. It should also be pointed out that all angular parts must be brought within the compact, curved shape of the body.

The head is an extension of the spine and as such must be included as part of the curve made by the rest of the body. Making this point to children attempting a forward roll for the first time will help most of them to achieve the skill smoothly and safely. Often when rolling children drop on to the back, which has been flattened as a result of the head, instead of the shoulders, first taking the weight. This can usually be overcome if the teacher leads the children to experience curving the spine and tucking the head while remaining in a crouch position on the feet. If, from this position, the hips are lifted and the feet push slightly, the head looking into the space between the legs, a roll will result. Others may find a roll over one shoulder easier and this can be achieved if, for example, from a position on all fours, the left hand is released and, with the head following, leads the body through the space made by the remaining hand and the knees. As the left shoulder comes level with the right knee, a state of unbalance occurs, and if weight is then taken on to this shoulder, an asymmetrical roll follows.

Some children will prefer rolling backwards over a shoulder, for once the hips are lifted off the ground and one or both knees directed over one shoulder, the balance of weight is such that the rest of the body naturally follows and a roll is achieved. For those who do not feel sufficiently confident to attempt either of these ways, rolling sideways, with the body either in the ball shape or elongated, will be their first experience of continuous movement using this method of weight transference. Another method of helping children to roll is to suggest they use the experience previously gained in rocking. Rocking on the back, for example, can lead quite easily, for some, into either a forward or backward roll, where the body shape remains constant. For those who quickly master rolling itself, combining rocking and rolling and exploring all the possibilities of rocking into and out of a roll provide a different challenge.

Plate 6

Plate 7

Plate 8

Plate 9

If the teacher suggests that rolling can be performed in a number of different ways and allows the class complete freedom to practise rolls already mastered, or to discover new ways of rolling, each child is able to attempt the way or ways he finds easiest. It is then left to the teacher, knowing all the possibilities and ways of achieving them, to lead the class or individuals gradually towards an appreciation of what is involved in rolling. Young children gain satisfaction from repetitive action and during the exploratory period it could be suggested that consecutive rolls are attempted. Most boys enjoy this activity, discovering that the rolls can take place within a limited area, *i.e.* a backward roll followed by a forward roll, or that travelling occurs when rolls are performed consecutively.

The more able the performer the greater the variety he should achieve, but each child, whatever stage he has reached, should be encouraged to perform asymmetrical rolls using right and left sides equally. Although most individuals have a preference for one side or the other, the ability to roll over either shoulder is of value later, particularly when performing a series of actions on apparatus or when working with a partner.

If sufficient mats are available when children begin work on rocking and rolling these should be used in the early stages, but as the action itself becomes more efficient and the children more confident, the necessity for mats diminishes and the tendency to limit the performer is avoided. Care is always needed whenever children roll without mats, and these should always be provided when using apparatus.

## 2. SLIDING

Although sliding is natural to most young children it is usually associated with an angled surface. It can, however, be experienced on the floor provided that it is clean and splinter free. This is an important point whenever children are working but even more so when the action involves friction.

The class should first experiment with actions which naturally terminate in sliding, *e.g.* when starting from a position on the floor with weight on hips, a vigorous pushing action of the feet against the floor will set the slide in motion. A more effective push, resulting in a longer sliding action, becomes possible if the weight is taken on the feet, body curled, and only when the legs become extended is weight transferred to the hips. Junior children are remarkably skilful at launching themselves on to the floor and into a slide. This can be experienced from a standing position or, as happens more naturally, from a run.

While experimenting with actions which result in sliding, children incidentally discover that many areas of the trunk can be used. They

E

can begin to combine the pulling and pushing action of the limbs with taking weight on different parts of the trunk, *e.g.* the weight can be taken on the front surface of the trunk and the hands used to pull and then push the body into a slide or, with weight on the hips, the hands and feet can push the body into action.

The more proficient children are, the greater the variety achieved. Most boys become expert at launching themselves on to the hips, front, side and thighs.

Some children naturally appreciate that the body travels better if it is streamlined and weight is taken on a comparatively small area. The teacher can help others to discover this by suggesting that they slide with whole surfaces of the body contacting the floor and then only part of this surface maintaining the body weight. In the latter instance the appropriate degree of bodily tension must be produced to hold the non-sliding parts off the ground.

3. STEP-LIKE ACTIONS

In step-like transferences many non-adjacent parts of the body can receive weight in turn. In rocking and rolling the child is concerned with large areas of the trunk along or across which weight is continually being transferred; now his attention is drawn to isolated parts of the whole body, and the combinations possible when using them in succession to produce locomotion.

It should be appreciated that in rocking and rolling movement will be continuous throughout the action. Step-like transferences may involve an interruption in the continuity of the action when weight is transferred on to flat or flattened parts of the body and maintained over that part for a brief period. This does not occur when the performer becomes more competent and able to repeat actions with ease and fluency.

The teacher should also realise that by the very nature of rocking and rolling activities, since adjacent parts are used in immediate succession, no variety of weight bearing parts is possible within one action. Step-like transferences, however, involve choice and therefore selection is necessary. It should be pointed out to the class that parts can be placed close to each other, as when transferring weight from feet to hands in a "Chinese" hand balance, or comparatively far away, as in a cartwheel. When the part which is being prepared to receive weight is to be placed to the side or a long way away from the supporting part, a considerable amount of bodily adjustment is involved, and great control is required before these skills are performed with any degree of fluency.

In some actions weight is taken from one part, received on another and placed back again on to the original part, as in handstands and cartwheels. Other actions can be accomplished which involve a constant change of parts receiving weight. In step-like transferences using hands and feet many variations are possible when combining the four limbs. The children should be allowed time to experiment, *e.g.* with transferring weight from two feet to two hands, two feet to one hand or from two hands to one foot. It is when dealing with step-like transferences of weight that the teacher should ensure that weight is taken frequently on the hands and in many differing situations. At an early stage in the Junior school, children should become increasingly confident in the inverted position. Tasks such as the following are challenges which will eventually lead most children towards becoming both competent and confident on the hands in inverted positions.

*Task* 1.—Take weight on to hands and make the legs land in a new place. Land one foot after the other, and two feet together.

*Task* 2.—Take weight on the hands and get one foot high into the air. (In this case the same foot will be used to push and land.)

*Task* 3.—Take weight on the hands and make one foot pass the other in the air. (This will involve one foot being used in the push-off and the other foot in landing.)

*Task* 4.—Take weight on the hands and make the feet meet at some point in the air. (One foot will be used to push off and the landing will be made either on two or one after the other.)

This method of transferring weight requires a studied, deliberate action on the part of the performer, and means that the child must think in advance of the action he is performing.

## 4. FLIGHT

Jumping is a natural action and children will have used it previously as a means of travelling, but when flight is being introduced as one of the ways of transferring weight some of the considerations which are involved in flight must be dealt with.

With young Juniors it is sufficient that they play with the various ways already used naturally, such as hopping, skipping, bounding and leaping. Later the teacher can make the class aware that the feet can be used singly or together in both take-off and landing; that feet can catch each other up as in a single take-off with two feet landing, or that feet can pass as in leaping from one foot to the other. Together with bouncing along on two feet or one foot these activities will involve them, incidentally, in the five basic jumps. At this stage it is the going away from and meeting the floor again that is emphasised, not being in the air.

The next stage will be to introduce the idea that individual parts of the limbs can be stressed after take-off, *e.g.* knees can be accentuated when the legs become freed, one or both can be tucked up towards the chest and this can be done together or one after the other; feet can be lifted high into the air in front of the body one after the other, kicked into the space behind, or brought to the side. It will be appreciated that although this task will result in a variety of body shapes being assumed in the air, shape itself has not been stressed. At this stage it is incidental and the attention of the class is directed towards awareness and use of different body parts. (*See* Plate 6.)

In the early stages of flight the accent should be on resiliency, as children are, on the whole, naturally more concerned with producing a succession of actions such as skipping or hopping. They enjoy experimenting with parts of the body other than feet on which they can bounce, and are prepared to choose activities involving shins, hips and shoulders. Bouncing, combining body parts such as hands and feet, can also be explored by some.

Within the jumping action the body spends such a comparatively short time in the air that the landing often occurs before any specific preparation or conscious effort can be made. In the transference of weight on to hands and feet, as in repetitive crouch jumps, the feet, which are usually both the ejectors and receivers of weight, are allowed more time in the air to prepare for the landing; consequently attention can be paid to meeting the floor. This slow motion effect of landing, for some, will be the experience they will find most valuable when considering the landing action. Weight should be received on to two feet or the feet used one after the other on landing, assuring equal efficiency in both methods of landing. As children become more proficient in flight and able to combine a variety of ways of transferring weight, *e.g.* run, jump, land and roll, they can be expected to produce appropriate ways of landing.

It is in the first two years with Juniors and the first year in the Secondary school that children should become thoroughly familiar with and skilful in ways of using the feet in take-off and landing. They should also have been given guidance in efficient ways of landing so that they feel confident in jumping from a variety of heights. Although the principles of landing are common to all, the teacher should be particularly aware of children who, through habit, lack of control or fear, land awkwardly. These individuals are always liable to have accidents, particularly as the flight becomes varied. Some children land with the feet wide apart, which could lead to damage to the knee. Others land with one or both feet slightly inturned, making ankle and knee liable to injury. A few children tend to assist landing on the feet with one or both hands, probably a continuation of young children's liking for landing on all fours. This could be dangerous, particularly when the weight is not directly over the feet and the hands are placed in front or behind in a misguided attempt to counteract the natural momentum and direction of the falling body. It is very difficult to break such habit actions so the teacher must deal with them promptly, before they become well established. These children need individual help and constant reminding of what they must do to correct such faults whenever landings occur in a lesson.

It is only by steering the children progressively through these early stages that the confidence required for the more advanced work will be gained and a real enjoyment of flight becomes possible.

This chapter covers only the elementary aspects of flight as a means of transferring weight; the three phases—take-off, period in the air and landing—are dealt with in greater detail in Chapter 12.

Although the teacher will guide his class through all the methods of transferring weight, only in the very early stages will these actions be performed in isolation. As soon as he feels the class capable of managing the body safely using one method, two ways of transferring weight at least should be combined. If, as previously suggested, rocking and rolling, and flight and sliding are introduced simultaneously, then choosing other appropriate ways is a natural progression.

With more experienced children the teacher should aim to foster the ability to build sequences, selected from the variety discovered, and to perform any combination of actions fluently.

## Apparatus

Work on apparatus challenges the children to perform types of action experienced on the floor at a variety of levels and on different surfaces, and to choose the appropriate method of transference of weight, so that movement over the apparatus becomes a logical and efficient way of travelling.

With Juniors just beginning this work, each method of weight transference should be explored separately. Apparatus should be provided where sliding, for example, is the activity which is emphasised, and although in order to slide down they must first climb up, sliding is the main action with which the teacher helps them to experiment. Climbing apparatus such as rope ladders, scrambling nets or wallbars allows the group to explore step-like transferences of weight. Although the hands and feet are naturally used when climbing, the class should be encouraged to try gripping with other parts. Juniors will provide a great variety of answers to the problem of showing flight either on and off or over apparatus. The teacher should help by ensuring that the apparatus is not too high at first. Where this is impossible, an inclined approach could be provided. He can suggest various ways of approach and encourage the group to use a number of different body parts to bear weight while fulfilling the task. (*See* Plates 7–9.)

The following tasks on apparatus could be given to a Junior or first year Secondary class who have just begun this work and need to experiment with each of the methods of transferring weight.

**Apparatus**—low table, or box top or form.

*Task.*—Find different ways to get on and off or over.

**Apparatus**—two inclined forms on Essex agility stools, with a linking bar.

*Task.*—Experiment with different ways of sliding—up and down the inclined forms and along the bar, either on top or underneath.

**Apparatus**—climbing frame.

*Task.*—Climb up, travel along and climb down, showing weight bearing on at least three different body parts.

**Apparatus**—steps or stage blocks.

*Task.*—Jump on and off or over.

**Apparatus**—mats.

*Task.*—Free practice in rolling, showing variety.

**Apparatus**—a series of canes supported on skittles.

*Task.*—Alternate jumping over and sliding under.

When considering apparatus for actions involving the transference of weight, the teacher should bear in mind that the four methods of weight transference can seldom be considered in absolute isolation. The following headings therefore consider two of the more usual combinations. The linking of like actions as in rocking and rolling should be taught first, as the transition is comparatively simple. Later, other combinations which include joining unlike actions, involving change of level for example, as in flight and rolling, can be attempted.

ROCKING AND ROLLING

These two actions can be performed over a low bar, on forms or low box top. It may be found that to cover the bar with a mat will provide a more comfortable surface on which to rock. The children can find ways of rolling along a form, forwards and backwards. They can experiment, using feet on the floor astride the form while the trunk rolls along the form, and complete the whole action with the body at the same level. The possibilities and advantages of rocking into rolling can also be explored. This activity will also involve the performer in skilfully balancing and controlling the body on the narrow surface provided by the form.

**Apparatus**—low box top, mats.

*Task* 1.—Get on to the box, roll along the top and jump off. Cross the mat using a different type of roll.

*Task* 2.—Get on to the box, roll along and off, and roll again on the mat.

*Task* 3.—Go straight from the floor into a roll on the box, rock off into a roll.

In the first task the roll will be completed on the same level, whereas in the second and third either the take-off or the completion will be on a different level from the roll itself.

STEP-LIKE ACTIONS AND FLIGHT

Getting on to apparatus at first usually involves step-like transferences in order to gain height so that flight may follow.

Using fixed wall bars, window ladders and double bars or apparatus such as the Cave Southampton, the tasks could be to climb up and jump down, or climb up, get through and jump down. The transferences here include negotiating comparatively small, vertical gaps. The children could also be expected to cover narrow, horizontal gaps where the level remains the same, *e.g.* two forms or two low box tops.

Apparatus such as the horse, box, buck or bar box can be used to get on using step-like transferences and get off by means of flight.

FLIGHT AND ROLLING

Rolling will have been practised at many of the earlier stages and can now be linked with landing from a jump. This necessitates an ability to move fluently from high to low level and involves a quick adjustment of body weight. It is, however, an essential skill and the class should be encouraged to explore with apparatus at a low height:

1. Landing and rolling in the same direction as the body weight. (This can be experienced jumping forward, backward, sideways and with the body turning.)
2. Landing and rocking.
3. Landing, controlling the body weight and re-directing the body into a roll.

The first two methods are the more usual and children should learn to feel where the body weight is on landing and act accordingly. Occasionally it is impossible to follow the natural direction, because of obstacles in the pathway of the mover, and the performer may be forced to resort to the third method.

It will be obvious from the above examples that many other natural combinations of transferring weight can be used, such as sliding into rolling, and step-like transferences into sliding. Eventually the class should be able to combine three or even all methods when using apparatus, if this has been arranged thoughtfully and with the theme in mind. The following examples could be used with Secondary children who have already been introduced to this movement idea and have experimented as suggested above.

**Apparatus**—an inclined form to a Cave Southampton side wall and a mat.

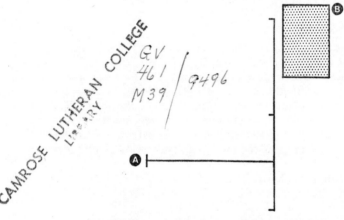

> *Task.*—Starting point A: a sliding action up the form; get through, along and jump down, roll over the mat.
> Starting point B: roll over the mat, climb up, travel along, get through and slide down.

**Apparatus**—bar box, two forms, two mats.

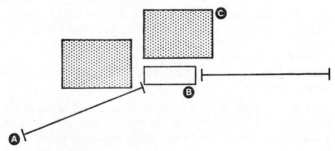

*Task.*—A, B and C show possible starting points. Take any starting point and show at least three different methods of transferring weight.

**Apparatus**—horse and two mats.

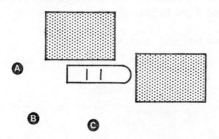

*Task.*—A, B and C are possible starting points. Approach from any angle, arrive on different body parts and get off using step-like actions; roll over mats.

**Apparatus**—a form inclined to a wall bar, two mats.

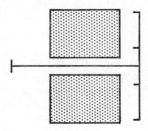

*Task.*—Use the apparatus with at least three ways of transferring weight.

**Apparatus**—a high bar and mats.

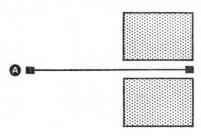

*Task.*—Starting point A. Travel along the bar (on top or underneath), using step-like and sliding actions, use flight to get off and a roll on the mat.

**Apparatus**—box, medium height.

*Task.*—Approach from any angle using a step-like transference to get on, and flight to get off.

**Apparatus**—low box and mattress.

*Task.*—Run, jump on to and off or over the box, land and roll.

**Apparatus**—horse, box and two mats.

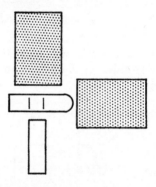

*Task.*—Include three ways of transferring weight within a sequence, using all the apparatus.

# CHAPTER 4

# INTERMEDIATE BODY MANAGEMENT

THEMES covered in the preceding chapter have stressed travelling and stopping, and the attention has been focused on specific body parts in action. The emphasis in stretching and curling, twisting and turning and symmetry and asymmetry is shifted to the consideration of the body as a whole; locomotion or stillness becoming incidental.

## STRETCHING AND CURLING

### Material

Once children have evolved various travelling possibilities and become familiar with ways of taking weight and transferring weight, the changing shape of the body whilst it is moving can be explored. The comparatively simple actions of curling and stretching will have been performed already many times, but without a conscious effort on the part of the child, whose attention will have been directed towards other problems.

Flexion and extension are integral parts of any action and common to all movement. Curling and stretching are basic movements of the spine and both are related to a centre, which in whole body movement would be the centre of the body. Stress differs, however, in that in curling it is to close around this area whilst in stretching the main aim is to reach out and away from it. In some instances, however, the pull away will be related to the base in addition to a centre as such. The stretching of the body when lying in an elongated position will be equally stressed in both the upper and lower halves, away from the central region, whereas the stretch experienced in a handstand will be felt as a pushing away from hands or base, although the feeling of reaching away from the centre should remain.

Over-stretching results in the body arching, and this can produce backward or lateral movements with one half of the body stretching while the other naturally compensates by contracting. In backward arching the front surface is extended while the back contracts, whereas when the sideways arch is achieved, it is one side of the body which is stretched while the other becomes compressed.

### Teaching

In all the previous ways of moving the body will have alternated between these two actions. Reference will have been made many times to both curling and stretching when rocking and rolling, while stretching will probably have been encouraged when dealing with certain aspects of flight. For a brief period it may be found valuable for children to experience the two extremes possible within this movement idea, in positions of stillness. Having to concentrate on rounding and elongating the spine and feeling its resulting effect on the whole body is useful as these two activities are obviously initiated in the trunk and awareness of this area is often neglected. Children should be guided towards feeling the positions of curled and stretched and also the process of becoming curled and stretched, appreciating the difference between "I am stretching" and "I am stretched."

If stretched and curled positions are achieved as the natural conclusion of stretching or curling actions, they can be of value in experiencing the ultimate. If children are merely expected to produce isolated stretched or curled positions the results will be relatively useless. It is the interplay and natural reaction of the body moving into and between curled and stretched positions that should be experienced. Static positions unrelated to each other are of little value, but the feeling of stretching and the differing sensation experienced in curling, and moving from one to the other are the important factors to be considered.

It should be realised at this juncture that in the action of stretching the body can be elongated, stressing the upper and lower halves reaching in opposite directions, or it can be wide, accentuating the right and left sides pulling away from the central line, the spine. In the very early stages of stretching or curling the trunk should be made the most important part of the body, as children readily achieve extension and flexion in the limbs but find mobility of the trunk a much more difficult task. The head, too, should be included in both these actions whether it is regarded as part of the trunk and an extension of the spine, or looked upon as another limb.

When children are being led through this first experience it is probably better for the teacher to suggest parts of the body which might take weight. It should be realised that only in positions of lying, standing on either feet or hands, and in the air, can a complete stretch be made, while curled positions can occur on feet, shins, either side and any part of the back. The whole class could quite quickly explore most of these possibilities, the majority being capable of experiencing all.

Having felt the extremes of curling and stretching with the body supported on bases selected by the teacher, the children can now experiment with other bases, symmetrical and asymmetrical, over which the rest of the body can extend or curl. It will be found that only an incomplete stretch is possible once the weight is taken on the shoulders or certain other parts of the body. Even so, when these bases are used the teacher should stress that the parts free and capable of stretching should do so to the full. Similarly, in curling it will be discovered that on certain bases one part of necessity will need to be extended, although the majority of body parts will be able to curl over this base.

The ability of the spine to curve and arch backwards, forwards and laterally must be exploited if true versatility and mobility are to be achieved. Often curling results only in forward and backward rolling actions, whereas if children are allowed to experiment with the idea that the spine is capable of arching backwards and sideways, the resulting variety of actions will be more productive as well as presenting a much more challenging task.

Most of this work will have been achieved statically and soon travelling should be stressed, as this necessitates weight being taken on various body parts, which will help the performer to experience leading into, moving through and resolving actions where the body is stretched or curled. The relation and interdependence of the two actions will also need to be discovered; that in order to extend, a preparatory flexion is required and that the natural reaction after a complete stretch is for the body to recover by contracting.

Travelling will probably include flight and it is here that the teacher should realise the difficulties involved in curling once airborne. It is much more natural to stretch in the air as, after take-off and in preparation for landing, the legs are already extended, while in an upward thrust the upper half of the body is automatically affected in the attempt to overcome gravity. Thus all the natural reactions of the body tend towards extension in the air and all the ways of stretching should be explored first before experimenting with curling the body in flight. Most children will find this difficult to achieve, as it involves a complete action taking place after take-off and before meeting the floor, and a deterioration in landing might result. It may be that the teacher will prefer to postpone this stage and cover it later in advanced flight.

## Apparatus

In the planning of apparatus for this theme the natural method of using the body should be considered, *i.e.* flexion usually both precedes and follows extension, the actions of curling and stretching thus alternating. It would be pointless to expect children to travel over several pieces of apparatus maintaining either a curled or stretched position, but the teacher should guide them to explore the many possibilities of stretching and curling according to the situations presented. It will soon be realised that in an action where the body is first curled and then extended, parts of the body may be stretched while others remain tucked. For example one part may be gripping the apparatus while the freed part reaches out to receive weight, as when swinging on a rope where the arms are flexed and the legs prepare to land, or when climbing a rope where the upper and lower limbs work alternately gripping, reaching, pulling and pushing.

Juniors can work with raised canes or hoops, individual mats and skipping ropes on the floor or forms and large mats, before attempting work on larger pieces of apparatus.

**Apparatus**—two individual mats.

    *Task.*—Cross A keeping the body curled, cross B stretching. Find your own way of joining the two movements.

**Apparatus**—two individual mats and two skipping ropes.

    *Task.*—Travel along the mats keeping the body curled, travel over the ropes going from side to side with weight on hands and the rest of the body alternately stretching and curling.

**Apparatus**—raised canes and hoops.

    *Task.*—Travel in, out and over, stretching and curling.

Forms and mats can be used with either Junior or Secondary classes.

**Apparatus**—a form used broadways.

    *Task.*—Travel across the form keeping the body tucked and return showing a stretch or arch.

**Apparatus**—a form used lengthways and a mat.

    *Task.*—Travel along the form alternately stretching and curling. Jump off the end and roll over the mat.

Tasks can be given to Secondary classes on individual pieces of apparatus.

**Apparatus**—a bar at hanging height.

*Task.*—Travel along either stretching or alternately stretching and curling.

**Apparatus**—a low bar.

*Task.*—Travel along jumping over and returning by rolling over or under.

**Apparatus**—ropes.

*Task. 1.*—Travel up (this will probably involve alternate stretching and curling).

*Task 2.*—Using one or two ropes explore the possibilities of changing shape whilst the ropes are still or moving.

**Apparatus**—climbing frame, window ladders or double bars.

*Task.*—Travel up and down, over or across with the body alternately stretching and curling.

**Apparatus**—box top or two layers of the box and mats.

*Task.*—Arrive on using hands and feet; get off with hands touching the mat first. (This task will result in the body curling on arrival and stretching to get off.)

**Apparatus**—horse and mats. Starting points A and B.

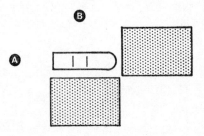

*Task.*—Arrive on and get off by taking weight on hands and achieving a stretch to land. Roll over either of the mats.

When children have had sufficient time to experiment on single pieces of apparatus, they can be presented with a more complicated arrangement where they explore curling and stretching possibilities before selecting a series of actions to be the basis of a sequence.

**Apparatus**—two forms, a buck and two mats.

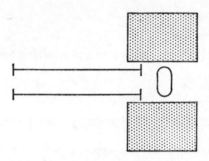

**Apparatus**—one form, two ropes and a box.

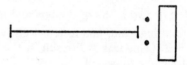

**Apparatus**—two bars, two inclined forms on the lower bar, two saddles and two mats.

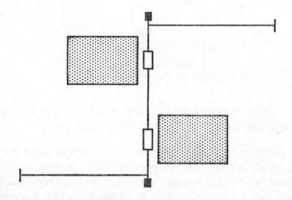

**Apparatus**—inclined form to a bar box, a horse with one pommel removed, two mats.

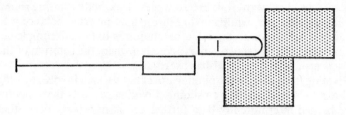

## TWISTING AND TURNING

### *Material*

Two further actions of which the body is capable are those of twisting and turning. Twisting is made possible because of the jointed nature of the body and if true mobility is to be encouraged then all the possible contortions of the trunk must be explored.

Twisting occurs when one body part is stabilised and the rest of the body screwed so that different surfaces face different fronts, *i.e.* parts of the body act in opposition producing torsion. Variety within the action of twisting is possible once the principle is established. The body may be kept compact and near the fixed part or it may reach away from the supporting area, thus providing opportunities for both curling and stretching while twisting.

A twist may be resolved either by releasing the fixed part, in which case turning usually results, or, once the twist has reached such a state that it can go no further, by allowing the body to recoil, the inherent speed changes involved in twisting becoming apparent. It will be found that movements leading into twisting are usually performed comparatively slowly, decreasing as the ultimate twisted state is reached, whereas the recoil will be explosive, with the initial burst of speed decreasing as the body returns to normal.

Different parts can be used to initiate a twisting action although eventually the whole body becomes involved. Often the part leading the body into a twist is the part that eventually takes and maintains weight. An effective way of preparing for a twisting action is to screw the body in the opposite direction first, when the release of tension will result in added impetus to the main action.

Turning concerns the body as a whole rotating at right angles about one of three possible axes—the up-down or vertical axis, and the two horizontal axes, the side to side and the forward-backward. Actions resulting from the body revolving around the vertical axis are limited in functional movement to those such as rolling with the

F

body maintaining an elongated position, spinning on the hips, turning jumps, or making quarter or half turns from a balance on hands. Forward and backward rolls are examples of the body rotating round the side to side axis, while moving through an inverted balance into an arch is an instance where the revolution is only half completed. A cartwheel will be recognised as an action where the rotation of the body is around the forward-backward axis.

Pivoting, swivelling and spinning are actions which involve turning and can be seen as similar to sliding. Pivoting suggests that impetus is recharged intermittently by a further action of a body part other than that taking the main weight. Swivelling or spinning occur when the initial action only is used to maintain the motion, which will eventually lose momentum and come to an end. The speed of the body can be varied to some extent in all these actions by the shape it assumes while rotating—a compact body will revolve at greater speed than when the body is spread. The surface areas used in pivoting, swivelling and spinning can be the same as in sliding. The flow of the movement in all sliding actions, whether on the spot or progressive, may be less bound than in many other gymnastic activities and provide moments when comparative free flow can be experienced and enjoyed.

Whereas turning is concerned with the body as a whole, twisting involves awareness of parts within the whole acting against each other. The fact that the body moves as a unit in turning permits simultaneous action only, whereas in twisting body parts are used successively, adjacent joints coming into action one after the other.

Unless use is made of twisting and turning actions the performer is limited to movement in the forward-backward and up-down directions. Twisting can result in static contorted positions being achieved with no further aim in view, but if the ability of the body to twist is exploited gymnastically then the action must become purposeful and objective.

In curling, stretching, twisting and turning the body is used to the fullest extent and if versatility is to be fostered all must be explored in depth. The ability to move fluently and with awareness, using appropriately these four actions both on the floor and on apparatus, is not easy to achieve, but when developed allows the performer a very much wider field of activity.

## Teaching

As with curling and stretching, if the teacher directs the first experience he can ensure that each child understands some of the fundamental principles involved within the action.

If twisting is not to become mere gesture, the teacher must ensure that it is used either to change direction, which involves weight being transferred on to another part of the body, or to gain initial impetus for a turning action or series of actions. In fact there is little point in twisting into a position and coming out of it again along the same path, once the initial feeling has been experienced. The following tasks put the children in twisting situations, and each is resolved by weight ultimately being transferred.

*Task* 1.—Start in a crouch position with weight on the feet, which are kept fixed. Use the hands to walk round the base until a position is reached where they can go no farther. Take weight on to the hands, release the feet and ground them again in a different place. (The teacher should ensure that twisting to both right and left is explored. A progression then is for the hands to be placed as far behind the body as possible and the twist resolved in the same way.)

*Task* 2.—Begin with weight on the shoulders with the legs extended symmetrically above the base. Draw both knees down over either the right or left shoulder and transfer weight, ending in a kneeling position.

*Task* 3.—Take up a kneeling position and place one hand on the floor. Allow the other hand to lead the body into the space between the fixed hand and the knees. Transfer weight on to one shoulder and either roll or maintain the weight over this base.

The class could now be given the task of discovering various ways of transferring weight from feet to hands and, by twisting, bringing the feet down in a different place. Here each child will solve the task in his own way and results may range from asymmetrical crouch jumps to variations of handstands and cartwheels with twists. Using their previous experience of rocking, some could now experiment with ways of twisting out of front rocking, where it will be discovered that if a quick twist is used either at the beginning or end of the action, weight can be transferred on to the back. The twist will occur when the weight is on the upper half of the body and the lower half is free to twist against it or vice versa.

Twisting can be combined with curling or stretching, when the body screws downwards towards the supporting base or the part which is eventually to take weight reaches away from the support. (*See* Plate 10.)

In turning the possibilities are varied but actions such as rolling will have already been experienced. This leaves only wheeling and spinning as new activities to be explored. The former is limited to actions where weight is borne alternately on hands and feet with the body wheeling over successive supports. Children should be given a brief experience of this way of turning. The resulting actions will develop, for some, into cartwheeling, for others, into unnamed wheeling skills.

Spinning, swivelling and pivoting on numerous parts of the body can be explored, with the children being encouraged to use twisting as a preparation for these activities.

Twisting and turning are easily linked as one often either precedes or results from the other. The opportunity to explore all the possibilities offered by both in objective work results eventually in the body being used in a skilful and versatile way.

Further aspects of twisting and turning are dealt with in the chapter on Flight.

## Apparatus

This theme should be introduced only when the class has covered all the previous movement ideas and is reasonably proficient at managing the body on apparatus.

**Apparatus**—mats and forms.

> *Task* 1.—Fix the hands and by releasing the lower limbs bring about a twist and a change of direction; on landing fix the feet and allow the upper half to initiate the twist and take the body weight. Repeat this and travel.
>
> *Task* 2.—Experiment with fixing other body parts on the apparatus and bring about twisting.

The teacher can, if necessary, suggest parts of the body to fix and encourage the use of the different levels provided by the form and the floor.

**Apparatus**—junior frames, wallbars both hinged and fixed, window ladders and single and double bars.

> *Task* 1.—Experiment with fixing parts of the body capable of gripping, *e.g.* parts of the foot, the back of the knee, the front of the hips, and waist.
>
> *Task* 2.—Travel up and down, along or across with a repetitive twisting action.
>
> *Task* 3.—Experiment with a variety of ways of rolling around the bars.

**Apparatus**—ropes.

> *Task* 1.—Experiment turning the body both forwards and backwards between two ropes.
>
> *Task* 2.—Swing on one rope, twisting and turning at the end of the action. (This will necessitate an active use of the lower half of the body.)

Individuals will invent their own methods of using one or two ropes to bring about twisting providing they have understood the principles involved.

**Apparatus**—horse, saddles, box and buck, used singly.

    *Task 1.*—Find ways of getting on and off showing a change of direction. (This will involve either a turn or a twist.)

    *Task 2.*—Get on and find ways of getting off so that the body finishes facing the apparatus. (This also, in most cases, will bring about either a twist or a turn.)

    *Task 3.*—Get on and jump off and roll, somewhere bringing about a twist.

When setting out more complicated apparatus it will help the groups initially if the apparatus is placed at angles.

**Apparatus**—form angled to a horse and a mat.

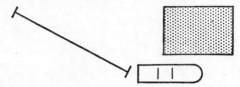

**Apparatus**—form angled to a box and a mat.

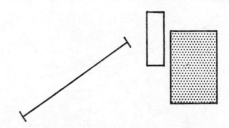

**Apparatus**—form angled to a bar box, ropes and a mat.

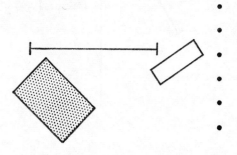

**Apparatus**—a low bar, one form inclined and one on the floor, two saddles and two mats.

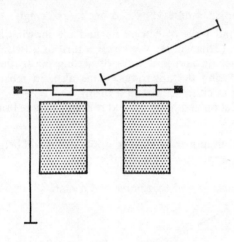

**Apparatus**—a bar at medium height, three forms, one underneath the bar, one inclined and one on the floor, two mats.

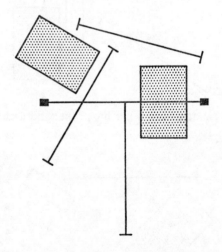

**Apparatus**—a form angled to the buck and a mat.

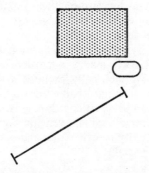

Tasks on such apparatus could be to use twisting actions:

(a) to negotiate corners or
(b) to bring about changes of direction while travelling.

### SYMMETRY AND ASYMMETRY
#### *Material*

Symmetry can be defined as equal proportions of the whole being distributed on either side of a line or plane into two or more parts exactly similar in size, shape and in position relative to the dividing points. Symmetry can be appreciated in the build of the body itself, the balance of parts being equal on either side, with the limbs arranged matching and in opposition in relation to the central dividing line of the vertebral column.

Although the body itself is symmetrical, the majority of actions performed are asymmetrical in detail. Eating, writing, walking are asymmetrical actions, where one side only is stressed or where the sides are used alternately. Rarely does one sit, stand or lie symmetrically although unlike writing and walking this is a possibility.

Symmetrical movement in gymnastics demands discipline, control, co-ordination and a keen sense of body awareness. Symmetrical locomotion is limited to the forward-backward direction and movements up and down, as any deviation from these leads into actions with a one-sided stress. In asymmetrical actions one side of the body becomes more active or a greater stress is laid on the right or left. This brings about unbalanced, lopsided actions where the body assumes irregular shapes, and all manner of twists and turns and changes of direction become possible. Twisting and turning are related to each other and both are associated with asymmetry. Turning about the side to side axis, however, is the only method of rotation where symmetrical or asymmetrical movement is possible. Turning about the up-down and forward-backward axis, where the body is divided into right and left sides will, of necessity, require one side to lead, an asymmetrical action resulting.

Experience of both symmetrical and asymmetrical ways of moving are valuable in that each makes a particular demand upon the performer. Moving symmetrically requires skill and an ability to manage the body in a stable, balanced way, where a feeling of precision and poise can be experienced. A greater variety of action is possible within asymmetrical movements, giving the inventive performer an opportunity to experience the one-sided stress and to master completely new skills.

## Teaching

This idea is rather more advanced than those previously taken, so that in the beginning it is dealt with in a very elementary way. Perhaps with Juniors the words themselves may not even be mentioned, other words such as "matching" "balanced", "even", "level," "lopsided," "odd," and "uneven" can be substituted. It will be found useful, however, to have covered the first stages of this concept before attempting more advanced work, as many progressions depend upon the performer being able to manage his body in both symmetrical and asymmetrical positions and to appreciate the relationship between this idea and twisting and turning, for example, or gaining and losing balance.

Initially each child can experience the symmetry of his own body by standing with weight equally distributed over both feet, appreciating the spine as the dividing line, the head being considered here as an extension of the spine, with the rest of the body matching on either side. Children can then be helped to explore other ways of achieving symmetry using a variety of bases. Within this task the body can be stretched, spread, rounded and arched. Symmetrical ways of travelling will be found and the limitations realised, among them that a double take-off only is allowed and that the body is restricted to the forward and backward direction and movements up and down. For many this will mean that balances on hands and head, and backward rolls previously achieved with a one-sided stress, must now be mastered in a new way, presenting a challenging situation to the more able.

Asymmetrical use of the body is simple to appreciate once the precision of symmetry has been experienced, the children realising that the former provides a much greater freedom of action. The teacher should be careful here to see that asymmetrical actions are always purposeful. For example, posing on the shoulders with one leg

PLATE 10.—Stretching and twisting

PLATE 12
A held body position
during asymmetric flight

Plate 12

Plate 13

PLATE 13.—A one-sided
stress leading to turning in
flight

stretched and the other bent is of little value, unless either the latter is being prepared to take weight in a backward movement or the body is going to be brought on to the feet and an asymmetrical placing is required for the following action.

It is useful to give the class the challenge of finding uneven bases which will probably involve an asymmetrical distribution of the rest of the body over the base.

Symmetrical and asymmetrical movement can now be linked and, for example, an inverted balance performed using an asymmetrical preparation achieving symmetry at some point and ending the action asymmetrically. The more able children could lead into the action with one leg following the other, achieve symmetry in the balance position and maintain the symmetry until the landing has been made. Relatively few will be able to perform the whole action symmetrically.

This theme is valuable in that clarity, precision and a heightened sense of body awareness are required and, although some will find symmetrical actions difficult to master, the discipline and control lead to true body management, one aim of gymnastics.

## *Apparatus*

In formal gymnastics many of the vaults were symmetrical, necessitating double take-offs and two-foot landings. The apparatus itself was usually placed symmetrically and in most cases the body followed a straight line in a forward direction.

Now, however, a blending of symmetry and asymmetry is encouraged to produce added variety and a more skilful use of the body when moving over apparatus.

Symmetrical movements on apparatus, as on the floor, are limited but require added control, balance and body awareness when working at the different levels provided by the apparatus. The possibilities of producing asymmetrical actions are greatly increased once apparatus is introduced as the variations in height can be exploited by asymmetrical grips and positionings.

In the first few lessons on this theme with Juniors it will be sufficient for the children to appreciate that the hands and feet can be used symmetrically and asymmetrically and they can experiment with ways of travelling along, up and down and over apparatus using one foot or two feet, one hand or two hands and also explore the possibilities of combining the symmetrical use of hands and asymmetrical use of feet, and vice versa. The task of travelling using two hands and two feet symmetrically along a form will probably result in the rest of the body moving symmetrically. In such cases the teacher could point out that in these actions not only do the limbs work symmetrically but the whole body travels with both sides matching. The class can then be given various pieces of apparatus to use such as climbing frames, ladders, planks, forms, steps, low box tops or stage blocks and challenged to travel symmetrically.

This method of moving on apparatus is too restricting for Juniors and so should not be pursued for long. The majority will probably grasp the main idea quite quickly and show both symmetrical and asymmetrical ways of travelling. Plates 11, 12 and 13 are illustrations of Junior boys showing asymmetrical flights.

Provided that adequate time has been allowed for exploration at floor level the work on apparatus can progress very quickly at the Secondary stage. Tasks on forms can be given which will guide the class towards appreciating that an asymmetrical base is possible using the two levels.

**Apparatus**—form used broadside uppermost.

> *Task* 1.—Travel along placing the hands symmetrically on the form. There is no need for the rest of the body to be symmetrical yet.
>
> *Task* 2.—Travel across and back again, using hands symmetrically on the form.
>
> *Task* 3.—Travel along and across, using alternate hands to take weight.
>
> *Task* 4.—Travel along or across, placing hands asymmetrically.
>
> *Task* 5.—Travel along or across, placing one hand on the form and one on the floor.

**Apparatus**—form narrow side uppermost. (It will now be impossible to grip the form using the hands symmetrically unless it is approached at right angles. Therefore all but the first of the above tasks can be repeated.)

Rolling symmetrically along forms forwards and backwards can be attempted. In some cases it will be found easier to achieve symmetry rolling along forms than on the floor, particularly if the feet and the trunk are at different levels.

**Apparatus**—mats.

> *Task* 1.—Cross the mat symmetrically and recross asymmetrically.
>
> *Task* 2.—Work out an asymmetrical balance sequence.
>
> *Task* 3.—Travel around the edge of the mat using symmetrical movements, progress forwards and backwards, and negotiate the corners asymmetrically.
>
> *Task* 4.—Approach the mat, cross and move away with matching and asymmetrical actions.

**Apparatus**—forms and mats.

*Task* 1.—Use both pieces of apparatus, showing symmetrical movements on one, asymmetrical on the other.

*Task* 2.—Using the form and mat together, achieve asymmetrical balance positions.

*Task* 3.—Jump over the form or use it to gain height. Gain symmetrical and asymmetrical body shapes in the air.

**Apparatus**—bar, hip height.

*Task* 1.—Cross the bar asymmetrically, recross symmetrically.

*Task* 2.—Cross asymmetrically, get under symmetrically.

*Task* 3.—Travel from one end to the other with asymmetrical movements on the bar and symmetrical movements on the floor.

**Apparatus**—double bars, low and medium height.

*Task* 1.—Travel up, over and down with a one-sided stress.

*Task* 2.—Use one bar to show symmetrical actions and the other asymmetrical actions.

*Task* 3.—Travel along using both bars together with a one-sided stress.

**Apparatus**—climbing frames.

*Task* 1.—Travel up showing symmetrical movements, through and down with asymmetrical movements.

*Task* 2.—Invent a sequence travelling symmetrically and asymmetrically alternately.

When planning apparatus the placement can do much to suggest the appropriate use of symmetrical or asymmetrical actions. Apparatus set in a straight line will probably lead to a predominance of symmetrical movements, particularly if the task is to keep on the apparatus. Skilled performers might, however, easily produce a completely asymmetrical sequence. Apparatus placed at angles and offering different levels will help the beginner to travel asymmetrically.

**Apparatus**—a low box with four mats.

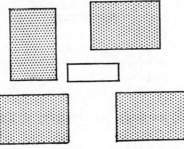

*Task.*—Arrive from a variety of angles, change direction to get off. Get on and off taking weight on hands, stressing symmetrical and asymmetrical use of hands and feet.

**Apparatus**—two forms leading up to saddles on a low bar and two mats. The apparatus is duplicated so that a group of six or more can be divided.

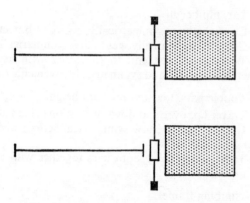

*Task.*—Travel using all the apparatus, including a return activity over the bar. Stress symmetry but achieve asymmetry at least once.

**Apparatus**—a set of ropes, mattress and two forms.

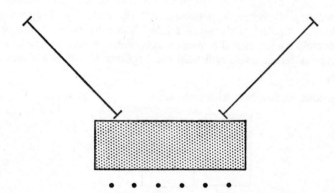

*Task.*—Take any starting point and, using all the apparatus, stress asymmetry.

**Apparatus**—a form leading to a low box, a horse and two mats.

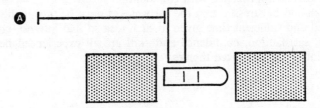

*Task.*—Starting at point A, use the form to show asymmetry and the low box to show symmetry, with a free choice over the horse and mats.

**Apparatus**—four ropes and a box.

*Task.*—Use assisted flight on to the box from any angle, transfer weight and achieve flight off the box. (Using two ropes often leads to symmetry, and one to asymmetry.)

**Apparatus**—two forms, one leading to a horse, the other angled, and two mats.

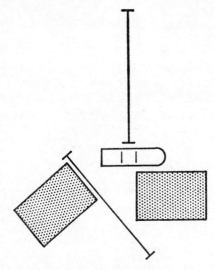

*Task.*—Use all the apparatus and negotiate the corners with asymmetrical actions.

This theme is ideal as an intermediate one as it revises work already covered yet demands greater skill, much care and thought.

If the elementary and intermediate themes are well taught the majority of children should reach the stage when the more advanced work can be approached with confidence.

It should be stressed that the early stages must be thoroughly explored and sufficient time given to each idea so that interest, enjoyment, satisfaction, confidence and skill are all experienced before presenting the advanced themes.

# CHAPTER 5

# CONTROL OF BODY WEIGHT, TENSION AND ENERGY

## *Material*

BODILY control in objective situations is one of the aims in gymnastics. In order to achieve physical mastery the child must learn to consider and manage his body weight and to produce the appropriate amount of tension and energy required in a variety of actions.

It is necessary to define some of the terms used in describing the body and the way in which it acts. The *kinesthetic sense* is the means by which changing muscular tensions are felt. The *weight* of the body is measurable and subject to the laws of gravity. The body produces *energy* which is the driving force behind movement. All movement involves a degree of resistance, whether this is produced within the body itself or from without by people or by apparatus. Resistance is overcome by using measurable degrees of *strength*.

### CONTROL OF WEIGHT

The control of body weight is one of the first considerations in gymnastics. The terms "weight bearing," "taking weight," "changing weight" and "transferring weight," suggest different movement possibilities but they have in common the necessity to feel and manage the weight.

Since the body is pulled downwards by gravity it is usually necessary to resist this and resulting actions range from maintaining an upright position to actually ejecting the body into the air. An awareness of the pelvic region, where the centre of gravity is normally located, is vital in all situations where weight is being considered.

Even in comparatively simple actions such as transferring weight from one base to another, management is important, particularly when the bases are far apart. The body must be held over the original base until the new one is prepared to receive weight, otherwise falling or collapsing might result. Control in such situations can also be achieved by the trunk and free limbs leaning or pulling away from the part that is to bear weight, counteracting the tendency to topple over, until the new base is ready. In balancing actions the free limbs can be used to counterbalance so that the weight is controlled and retained over the base.

In some actions the weight is instrumental in bringing about a change of situation. The impetus in swinging can be gained and re-charged by an active use of the body weight. Similarly, positions of balance are often lost by deliberately moving the centre of gravity so that it falls outside the base.

Once a certain degree of control is attained and the body weight can be guided safely and used effectively, it is profitable to experiment with tipping, tilting or leaning actions. In these situations the weight can be shifted gradually so that, in order to avoid falling, locomotion takes place. If the weight is "let go" and caught again its role in stability and mobility can be recognised and exploited.

It is more difficult to control the weight at take-off, while the body is in the air, and when it meets the floor again, than in purely earth-bound situations.

## CONTROL OF TENSION AND ENERGY

When muscular tension is present the body is active whether it is moving or holding a position. Lack of tension results in heaviness. The latter state taken to its extreme is the antithesis of movement and bodily control. Gathering tension produces gripping in the whole or parts of the body, while decreasing tension leads to relaxing.

In all gymnastic actions muscular tension is present but in some it is particularly important. When balancing, the body is kept over the base and this implies that a certain degree of tension is produced. In holding a balanced position the body should have sufficient tension to maintain an upward stress rather than a weighty, downward one. Actions concerned with a poised arrival on apparatus, especially from flight, involve varying degrees of tension. This enables the movement through space to be arrested and the body to achieve stillness, so that a balance can be maintained.

In working on the floor the latter provides the resistance against which the body pushes in order to lift or jump and to which the body adapts on landing. Contacting the floor, apparatus or people demands a changing output of energy. Gripping, releasing, pushing, pulling, ejecting and landing are examples of actions in which certain degrees of energy are inherent.

In gymnastics the energy expended is often considerable, particularly in apparatus work where obstacles have to be mounted or cleared. For any type of jump to be effective there must be an outburst of energy. Similarly the release of a full twist, the slashing action of the legs to turn the body when swinging on a rope, the whipping action of the free limbs to cause loss of balance, the pressing of the hands against the floor or apparatus during inversion, all are characterised by the strength required for efficient performance.

Actions requiring a weaker output of energy are less common and generally occur when the body is poised on apparatus, in some pin-point balances, and while the body is in the air.

The body must be involved as a unit when producing energy, whether the result is manifest in actions of the whole body or an isolated part. Because the hips are associated with the centre of gravity it is essential that the lower half of the body is used to maximum effect when strong actions are required. The upper half of the body, particularly the head and chest, become important in actions where the energy output is slight.

An awareness of the changing tensions and the differing amounts of energy which the body can produce is vital to the gymnast. Without this awareness the work might be bodily competent but lacking in vitality and interest.

In gymnastics there is a certain association between the rate at which the body moves and the amount of energy expended. The most usual combination is seen in strong, quick actions. Inverting the body, getting off the ground and on to or over high apparatus usually necessitates a strong action which, in order to be effective, must be executed quickly. This combination of speed and energy gives the characteristic zest to gymnastic action.

## Teaching

All movement involves body weight and, to a greater or lesser degree, tension and energy. Therefore, this is not a theme to be taken over a series of lessons but should be an ever-present consideration of the teacher, who in turn leads the children progressively towards a similar understanding. The relevant aspects of weight, tension and energy are discussed in each specific theme but it is profitable to see how the teacher can develop these throughout the work as a whole.

In the elementary stages children are given varied experiences which are aimed at awakening and enlivening their kinesthetic sense. The awareness and control of the body weight is an intrinsic part of this fundamental work. Locomotion, stillness, weight bearing and weight transference are situations in which management of weight is the prime concern. Children's physical growth should always be taken into account; height, weight and proportions alter, so the teacher cannot expect that once control is gained at any particular stage it will remain. Because of this and the fact that new situations are presented as the work progresses, control of weight is an aspect of movement to which the teacher should often refer.

In curling, stretching, twisting and turning, children must feel the different tensions which make these actions what they are. The weaker tension and inward focus of curling should be contrasted with the two-way outward pull of stretching, the radiating tensions of spreading

G

and the varying stretched and compressed tensions within twisting. The teacher must ensure that children experience these tensions often and to the full, for the particular tensional "feel" associated with an action should be remembered and retained, so that it becomes a part of the movement experience that can be reproduced accurately when required. Symmetry, asymmetry and body shape in stillness and when moving are also achieved by muscular tensions and the bodily "feel" is again important. Once children can consider and control the changing tensions within their bodies their work becomes livelier and clarity of movement is possible.

Although output of energy has always to be considered in gymnastics the first time this is stressed is probably when flight is introduced as a way of transferring weight. In all jumping activities, particularly in bouncing, where resilient recoveries are important, considerable energy is needed. With Juniors, whose energy seems limitless in this respect, the teacher has an excellent opportunity to make certain that these activities are fully experienced so that they can later be extended and built upon.

In order to tackle the more advanced themes children must have acquired a degree of bodily mastery which includes control of weight and the ability to select appropriate tensions and output of energy. Management of weight and tension is necessary in moving slowly, whereas quick actions demand much energy. In helping children achieve continuity of action the teacher must realise that it is only when weight, tension and energy can be controlled and used effectively that a blending of adjacent actions is possible.

When children work with a partner or within a group they are often in a situation where they have to cope with the weight of others, and this entails producing comparatively great degrees of strength. Before tackling the advanced themes of balance or flight the teacher should appreciate that the former is more concerned with weight and tension while in the latter it is the energy involved that is stressed.

The resistance and firm base provided by the asphalt playground and the wooden floor are accepted but rarely used consciously. Just as apparatus can be considered as an extension of the floor, in this respect the floor should be used as a piece of apparatus. One way of developing sensitivity is to set "touch before contact" tasks. In these the body part about to receive weight briefly touches the floor prior to being placed ready for weight bearing.

### Apparatus

Teachers will appreciate that the activities suggested in Chapter 1 as the basis for selecting apparatus all involve, to a greater or lesser extent, an ability to control the body weight, the necessity to select suitable tensions and the appropriate expenditure of energy for efficient performance. There must always be an awareness of these aspects when answering any apparatus task, even though the main consideration may be directed elsewhere. When the teacher realises that efficiency of action is impaired through lack of appreciation of weight, tension or energy, specific tasks such as those involving pushing, pulling, gripping and swinging could be given.

CHAPTER 6

# THE USE OF SPACE

## *Material*

THE individual's interest in space is twofold. Firstly, his attention can be focused on the space immediately surrounding the body, which is within his reach by normal extension. Secondly, the space shared by others and confined only by the walls of the gymnasium or playground or broken and sectioned by apparatus, can be equally important.

In the following ideas the focus of attention is on *where* the body is moving. In gymnastics movement follows either a straight or roundabout *path*, and at any time during locomotion, the body can be moving in one of three *directions* and at one of three *levels*. The *shape of the body* in space is constantly changing and this can be considered in both locomotion and stillness.

## 1. PATHWAYS

Locomotion is one of the main concerns in gymnastics and although the first consideration is body stress, the track made when travelling is inextricably linked. At floor level, pathways involving the general space are immediately dictated by obstacles in the way of the mover. These may be mobile or stationary; mobile in the case of others also working in the general space, stationary when the deviations in track necessitated by walls, railings or projections are considered.

While travelling the body can move in a straight line, or along straight lines producing angular floor patterns, or can swerve and twist following a circuitous route. The relation between straight pathways and the symmetrical use of the body can be appreciated as well as the connection between twisting, asymmetry and the resulting indirect tracks. The course followed over apparatus can also vary, with special attention being paid to angles of approach and methods of leaving the apparatus.

The floor and air patterns resulting from travelling actions will usually be incidental, but a growing awareness and ability to move fluently should be stimulated, and the conscious following of a variety of pathways encouraged.

## 2. DIRECTION

When considering direction the attention is focused on the space immediately surrounding the body into which a part or the whole is about to move. The main directions in which the body travels in gymnastics are forwards, backwards and sideways and these are closely linked with stability. Deliberately moving into a diagonal direction is associated with certain aspects of flight and loss of balance where momentary instability is experienced.

A change of direction can be brought about in two ways. The body can move forward, backward and then sideways.

1. with no change of front or
2. continuing along a straight path, each action linked by a turn or twist.

When studying the relationship between twisting, turning, symmetry, asymmetry and change of direction, certain links can be established.

*Symmetrical* travelling is limited to the *forward* and *backward* directions, while moving *asymmetrically* allows the body to perform actions in all directions including those to the *side* and along the *diagonal.*

*Twisting* brings about continuous *changes of direction. Turning* about the *vertical axis* allows a *change of front* to occur.

*Turning* about the *side to side axis* limits the movement to a *forward and backward direction. Turning* about the *forward and backward axis* brings about actions to the *side.*

## 3. LEVEL

When changes of level are observed it is the body as a whole which must be studied. Actions which elevate take the body *high* into the space beyond the normal reach, while those which keep the body moving near the floor involve travelling at the *low* level. The *medium* level in gymnastics is relatively unimportant and tends to be "moved through" rather than stressed.

## 4. BODY SHAPE

The shape the body makes while travelling or in stillness is, at times, incidental. An awareness of the body outline in space and consequent shape, however, can often help clarify actions.

When curling, stretching, arching and twisting occur it is the actions that are stressed, the shape of the body remaining of secondary importance. Once the action becomes part of the movement vocabulary, a progression can be recognised when the shape of the body assumes a greater importance and the attention of the performer can be directed towards the body contour. It is here that the arch achieved in a backbend can be fully appreciated, the wide, extended star shape of the cartwheel more defined and the elongation of the body in a handstand perfected. This is the stage when definition of shape adds clarity of line to an action and a positive attitude towards the body shape in space can be adopted.

The difference between movements where the body shape is maintained throughout the action, as in cartwheels and rolls, and those where a specific shape is only momentarily achieved, as in a handstand, can be observed.

The shapes that the body can assume while airborne can be explored. It has already been stated that stretching is simpler than tucking, but both are possible. Twisting and turning where changes of direction and front occur can also be achieved if anticipated in the take-off.

Apparatus limits the space and provides barriers to get over, under, in and out, through and round. In manœuvring the body the shape is constantly changing, always adapting to the new situations presented by the apparatus.

## Teaching

These themes are essential if children are to appreciate and become aware of themselves in relation to others or apparatus. It is also important if they are to become adept at judging heights and distances relative to the body. In both cases it can be seen as a vital safety factor when children are moving in the gymnasium or playground. The awareness of both personal and general space is necessary if these are to be exploited, variety achieved and the body used to its fullest extent.

### 1. PATHWAYS

*Juniors.*—When travelling on feet the natural reaction of young children is to move around the hall or playground following a circular track and moving in a forward direction. If, however, they begin facing one other person they can be given the task of running, dodging and swerving to avoid others. This starting position is one way of ensuring that individuals will be facing different directions and when travelling commences an avoiding action must immediately be taken. When other tasks have been answered involving locomotion, often a greater variety can be achieved if the attention is drawn to the floor patterns created. The teacher may dictate the track or the class may be left free to invent their own. The patterns shown at the top of the following page are but a few from which a selection can be made.

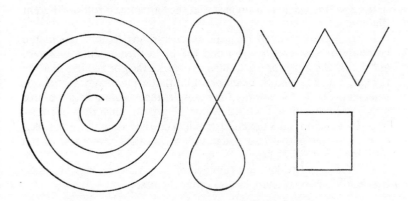

Juniors enjoy the challenge of producing recognisable floor patterns while travelling. It should be noted that direction and level of work are unimportant at this stage: it is the pathway that is stressed.

Suggested tasks linking locomotion and track:

*Task 1.*—Travel on hands and feet, making a zig-zag path.
*Task 2.*—Travel on parts of the trunk, creating a curved pathway.
*Task 3.*—Roll, making a circular track on the floor.

*Secondary.*—Older children could also work on this idea but it would not be necessary to dwell on pathways at floor level. The teacher could draw attention to the possibilities and refer incidentally to this when dealing with later themes and when working on apparatus. Air tracks could be explored with some classes, stressing the long, low trajectory required for length or the high, curving course needed if height is to be gained. Twists and turns while the body is upright in flight can be experienced by all, while actions where the body rotates about other axes in space can be attempted by the few. Following a track made by a partner is fully covered in the chapter on Partner Work.

## 2. DIRECTION

This aspect of space has an obvious link with the elementary body management themes and can be considered at any stage, once the main idea has been grasped. If, for example, locomotion with moments of stillness has been taken, once the majority have grasped what is involved and are able to bring this about, an added task of change of direction can be given. The challenge could be that after each pause a change of direction takes place.

When children have experimented with rolling actions, it would be natural for the teacher to suggest that they attempt to roll in different directions.

It can be appreciated that the teacher needs to understand the correlation between direction and the main theme being explored, and know the appropriate moment to make the connecting link for the children. It needs to be emphasised that a mere comment is not sufficient. The verbal noting, for example, that twisting brings about a change of direction, is of little value. This point must then be translated into action, and the children allowed time to explore the idea anew, with the added knowledge influencing their awareness of the movement possibilities.

The following tasks are examples of how the link can be made between directional changes and other themes.

*Task* 1.—Starting on the feet, transfer the weight onto the shoulders. Find three ways of answering this task, showing movement into different directions.

*Task* 2.—Invent a sequence which includes stretching, arching and curling—each action must lead the body into a different direction.

*Task* 3.—Choose three actions which take the feet into the air. Bring about a change of direction by turning or twisting out of these positions.

*Task* 4.—Run and jump, turning in the air so that on landing a backward or sideways roll results.

3. LEVEL

Locomotion involves the body moving in one level or another, but when exploring this idea the stress is mainly on extending the normal range; getting as high or as low as possible and experiencing the transitions when moving easily through all three.

Juniors enjoy pulling and pushing themselves along the floor, slithering and sliding, keeping very near to the ground. They delight in leaping and throwing themselves to the floor or launching themselves into space. They revel in space and need a sufficient area to experience this freedom.

Secondary classes seem less inclined to exploit the space; few experience the exhilaration of true flight or enjoy moving very near to the ground. Although the latter is understandable, the former warrants question. Several factors can be seen to influence the confidence of the Secondary child. He becomes heavier, taller, experience has taught him fear, while self assurance is often undermined by well-meaning parents and teachers. Yet another relevant point to be taken into account is that in the last year of the Junior school, examination work often takes time-table priority, and organised physical activity is unfortunately neglected, resulting in loss of agility.

In the Secondary school the three phases of flight must therefore be handled carefully, and particular attention given to safe landings and efficient take-offs if confidence is to be restored. It is essential that children move fluently and without restraint at any level, and tasks involving leaping and rolling, including turning in the air and change of direction, springing on to the hands and dive rolls, should be given. The teacher must ensure that children move confidently from one level to another on the floor before expecting work on this idea to be attempted on apparatus other than forms.

### 4. BODY SHAPE

The concern of the teacher should be to ensure that the facility with which actions are performed is such that the attention is no longer devoted to the skill but can be directed towards the shape of the body as it moves in space.

An awareness of body shape can be introduced by demanding clarity of position at the beginning and end of a sequence. When children have experienced weight bearing or balance, the shape of the body over the base can be clarified and the action repeated exactly. A clear shape is required by the person producing the obstacle in partner work. It will be realised that all the above examples occur when the body maintains a still position and the shape can be held.

With older, more experienced classes, a heightened awareness of the body in motion, on floor level and in flight, can be aimed for. The changing body shapes in cartwheels and catsprings, for example, can do much not only to clarify the action but actually help the performer master the skill.

Shape can readily be appreciated through observation of others. The teacher should take advantage of this by including short sessions in the introductory stages. Thus what is meant by shape can be seen, understood and implemented in the child's own work.

## Apparatus

### 1. PATHWAYS

Pathways over apparatus are at first incidental to the actions performed but tracks become increasingly important as variety of approach and inventive use of apparatus are stressed.

Pathways can be influenced by the arrangement of apparatus— the two examples below suggesting the obvious, but not necessarily the only, pathway.

**Apparatus**—spring board, box, rope and mat.

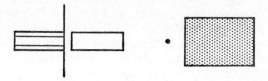

**Apparatus**—form inclined to the bar box, horse and mat.

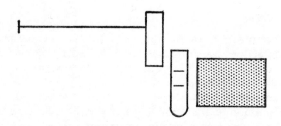

It should be noted that placement of spring boards, forms and mats particularly, does much to dictate possible starting and finishing points.

Tracks can be dictated by the teacher in the task set, regardless of the placement of apparatus, as in the following example:

**Apparatus**—form, low box, horse and mat.

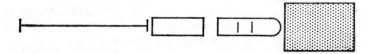

*Task.*—Travel over the apparatus making a zig-zag track. N.B. This will involve moving on and off or diagonally over the apparatus.

A number of tracks should be provided by the arrangement so that individuals may choose their own, but the groups should be kept small so that, if desired, all may work at once. One example is given opposite of such an arrangement.

**Apparatus**—ropes, two bars, one form inclined to the high bar and the other flat, a spring board, box and horse.

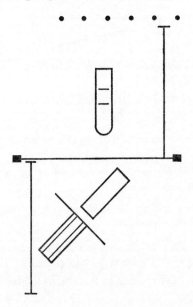

When stressing pathways attention should be drawn to spaces between apparatus, and the use of the floor in linking actions. If this point is not appreciated the continuity of action over apparatus is often interrupted and disjointed. At an early stage children should be encouraged to use floor space. Return activities using the floor can be suggested if apparatus is limited, *e.g.* when using forms only the challenge might include a floor task. With Junior classes small apparatus placed on the ground helps to direct their attention to possible paths, as in the following examples.

**Apparatus**—a form and four individual mats.

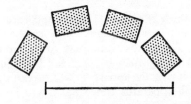

*Task.*—Travel along the form making an angular path and over the mats moving along a curved track.

**Apparatus**—form and two skipping ropes.

> *Task.*—Travel along the form and return using either rope showing a clear change of path.

The air tracks can be highlighted when clearing apparatus, by repetitive actions involving flight.

**Apparatus**—three forms placed at regular intervals and used broadways.

> *Task.*—Run and jump over or on and off each form producing repetitive air patterns.

A variation of this task could be to provide a situation where both height and length are included.

**Apparatus**—two layers of the box leading to a high bar, the box so placed that flight is necessary onto the bar.

> *Task.*—Run and use the box to leap on to the bar, swing and drop on to the floor.

Air path can be stressed when swinging on ropes, where the track the body makes through the air can vary. If the body is taken into the air and released from the rope at the highest point, the air pattern is different from that made by the body if it swings into the air and is released only when the feet touch the floor at the lowest part of the swing.

Once this aspect of space has been dealt with it can be referred to whatever the main theme of the lesson. The teacher can expect the class to become increasingly conscious of the variety of pathways possible on apparatus, and to select specific tracks relevant to the situation.

## 2. DIRECTION

The most natural way of travelling on apparatus is to move forwards and this must be taken into account when setting tasks which dictate direction. Apparatus which has to be mounted or cleared must of necessity be approached with the body moving forwards, but once in contact with the apparatus a change of direction can take place. Leaving the apparatus can equally well be effected moving backwards or sideways.

Apparatus such as bars, ropes and window ladders provide ample opportunity for moving in all directions, including the diagonal.

Flight into any direction can be experienced from forms, spring boards and trampettes and with the more skilled classes flight into the diagonal can be attempted.

Tasks on apparatus can ensure that the beginner experiences moving in all directions:

**Apparatus**—three mats.

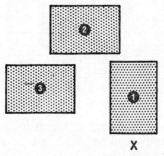

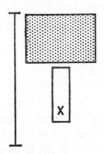

*Task.*—With X as the starting point, work over all three mats, forwards over mat 1, sideways over mat 2 and backwards over mat 3.

**Apparatus**—a form and mat.

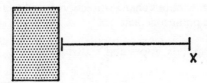

*Task.*—Begin facing the form at X.—Cross and recross the form travelling forwards and backwards; move sideways over the mat.

**Apparatus**—box top, mat and form.

*Task.*—Starting at X, move backwards over the box, sideways across the mat and forwards along the form.

**Apparatus**—spring board or trampette and mats.

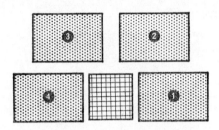

*Task.*—Using the spring board or trampette, run jump and land. At the first attempt land on mat 1 and from subsequent jumps land on 2, 3 and 4 in turn.

When children have explored the various possibilities of moving in different directions much more freedom can be given.

**Apparatus**—high and low bar.
   *Task.*—In three actions change direction, using each bar separately and at one point together.

**Apparatus**—form, box, ropes and mattress.

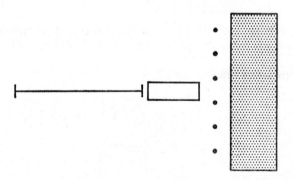

*Task.*—Start at the end of the form and travel to the mattress changing direction twice. N.B. It would be possible to get diagonal flight on to the outer ropes from either end of the box.

**Apparatus**—spring board, buck, ropes and mat.

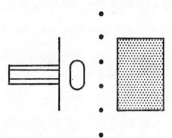

*Task.*—While travelling, bring about changes of direction by twisting and turning.

## 3. LEVEL

Once apparatus is introduced, level becomes a dual consideration. The level on which the body is moving relative to the apparatus, and the height of the apparatus itself, are often confused. Working in contact with apparatus which is at a height from the floor does not mean that the body is moving in the high area, although a feeling of being high is naturally experienced. Negotiating the body onto the high apparatus may have included flight but this need not necessarily be so.

Taking the body into the area high above can be explored using steps, stage blocks, low tables or box tops, forms, spring boards and trampettes. Inclined forms or planks to stools, bar box or bar can be used once the class has the confidence to exploit these situations. If the task involves jumping from too great a height too soon, the action will become one of dropping. Anticipation of landing will occur and rather than reaching into the space above, height is lost even before leaving the apparatus.

The ability to land from a height with a deep drop should be encouraged and the skill involved in moving easily from that position either into a roll or to rebound resiliently should be mastered.

In the following examples of apparatus and tasks, the level is dictated, but whenever apparatus is being planned the teacher should keep in mind that level is an important factor.

**Apparatus**—hoop held parallel to the ground by a partner, or a cane raised on skittles.

*Task.*—Run and leap high into or over the hoop or over the cane and return low by sliding or rolling underneath.

**Apparatus**—individual mats.

> *Task.*—Run and jump high over the mat, return keeping near to the ground.

**Apparatus**—form.

> *Task.*—Travel from side to side, alternately using the form to gain height and return keeping low.

**Apparatus**—form and mats.

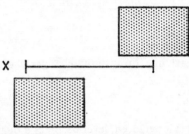

> *Task.*—Starting at X, move over the form and mats showing a change of level.

**Apparatus**—bar and mats; height of bar to be determined by the height and ability of the group.

> *Task.*—Run and jump to reach the bar, land and roll across the mat.

**Apparatus**—inclined form on to a low bar and mat.

> *Task.*—Run and jump off the form, roll across the mat and return over the bar, keeping the body near to the apparatus.

**Apparatus**—trampette, trapeze, high bar and mattress.

> *Task.*—Show changes of level while travelling over the apparatus.

**Apparatus**—two layers of the box, trampette, ropes and mattress.

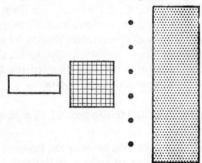

*Task.*—As above. N.B. This arrangement offers greater scope for the more skilled performer and can be made progressively more difficult by

(*a*) raising the box,

(*b*) increasing the distances between box and trampette and trampette and ropes,

(*c*) encouraging diagonal flight from the trampette to the end ropes.

## 4. BODY SHAPE

This has to be taught with understanding otherwise static "poses" appear with the held shape bearing no relation to the arrival or method of leaving the apparatus. As in floor work the shape of the body can be considered in stillness or while travelling. Unlike work at ground level, however, the shape of the body is often dictated by the outline of the apparatus itself and by the spaces presented.

Children can more readily appreciate shape when the body remains in the normal upright position, and ropes, bars and wall bars provide situations where this is possible. It is a distinct progression when re-orientation in inversion is such that attention can be directed towards body shape. This stage can be reached more easily if teachers realise that some apparatus such as ropes, bars, window ladders and parallel ropes provides many points of support. These offer opportunities for the body to be held in or moved into the inverted position, affording a degree of security not always experienced on portable apparatus.

Once balancing on apparatus has been mastered, the teacher could turn the attention of the more able children to the held shape. This not only provides a further challenge but helps the performer achieve a greater clarity of movement, resulting in more finished work.

Apparatus which assists take-off allows the performer a greater time in the air to achieve, establish and feel body positions. Ropes and bars are ideal apparatus upon which changing body shapes can be experienced while travelling. A more advanced stage is reached when the performer is so competent while moving on and clearing apparatus that awareness of body line can be noted and appreciated.

Most of this work is for the skilled performer and those who are more spatially conscious than others. It is essentially a theme for Secondary classes although some ten year olds would be capable of tackling a few of the simpler ideas suggested.

Secondary boys are usually much more interested in acquisition of skill; body line and finished work is often neglected, but for the advanced gymnast, work on this could produce a much higher standard of performance.

H

No specific tasks or arrangements of apparatus are given as this idea can develop from work already being produced on other themes such as weight bearing, balance or flight. It is for the teacher to recognise when an individual is capable of accepting the additional challenge, and set tasks accordingly.

CHAPTER 7

# CHANGES OF SPEED

## *Material*

THE gymnastic themes considered so far have included a concern for awakening the kinesthetic sense, and the attention has been directed towards *what* the body is doing in any action. In this new movement idea the focus is on *how* the action is being performed.

In order for movement to take place a degree of speed must be present, and in gymnastics the rate at which the body moves is explored. This is the speed aspect of the motion factor of Time. It is measurable and objective and it has two integral elements—quick and slow. Both are easily distinguishable, with recognisable varying degrees between the two extremes.

Within most actions or series of actions, time changes are obvious, resulting in certain stresses, rhythms, accelerations and decelerations. Some gymnastic actions are, by their very nature, concerned with one element rather than the other. The speed inherent in the action of ejecting the body into the air, for example, is obvious; if a leap is to be effective then a quick, energetic use of the body is required. If, on the other hand, a balance is to be achieved, usually the point of equilibrium is reached by the body moving relatively slowly into position. Other actions can be performed at a variety of speeds depending upon the degree of proficiency already acquired. Activities such as rolling at different speeds can be attempted by the majority of children, although comparatively few will be able to perform cartwheels using more than one speed.

Within a single action time changes are often apparent; a handstand, for example, normally consists of a quick action to invert the body, a deceleration as the body becomes balanced over the hands and an acceleration as the feet return to the floor.

In the majority of sequences changes of speed become even more evident. When moving fluently from one action to another it is important to appreciate the appropriate use of speed and to acquire the physical ability to perform actions at a variety of speeds. Formal gymnastics stressed quick movement, with the climax placed in the middle or towards the end of each series of actions. The main action was usually concerned with clearing apparatus and this naturally necessitated acceleration. The landing, often assisted and controlled by supports, was abrupt. Therefore the rhythm in vaulting was, generally, acceleration into the main action and stop.

As gymnastics is taught now, many essential differences immediately present themselves. In formal work on apparatus a pre-selected series of actions only was possible, which involved a narrow use of speed. In modern work the many gradations are explored. This is made possible by the variety of ways in which the apparatus is used. While at times a single action only is required, more often the challenge is such that the apparatus may be used more than once, or a sequence of movements performed using several pieces of equipment. This requires the performer to vary his speed over the apparatus, to blend recovery and preparation and to adapt his timing to the situations presented.

Another obvious difference between the two ways of teaching gymnastics is that, in the formal method, the individual's time preference was completely disregarded and only those who naturally inclined towards quick, direct, energetic actions were catered for. In modern gymnastics the tendency for individuals to move with a characteristic time stress is recognised. Although at first this is allowed to predominate the teacher should ensure that each child not only recognises the range possible within this theme but is encouraged to extend his own to the limit. In this respect working with a partner is invaluable, since individuals are placed in the situation of moving with new time stresses, enlarging their speed vocabulary in the process.

When exploring the play between the two extremes of *quick and slow* it is natural to consider *acceleration* and *deceleration*. The ability to bring about an increase and decrease of speed quickly or gradually is an important safety factor in any gymnastic situation. It is also essential that the skill involved should be mastered, so that work on apparatus can be fully enjoyed and heights gained and distances covered with confidence. Acceleration or deceleration can best be experienced, in the first instance, by repetition of a single action, but can also be accomplished within a single action or within a sequence.

Both gaining and losing speed can produce highlights during a series of movements. A *climax* need not necessarily always be associated with quick, strong or elevated action but could be the moment which the performer wishes to stress, or when the main objective is achieved. This point may be reached once or several times and can be placed anywhere within the sequence. When working at floor level the choice of accent is governed only by the task set, and the performer is comparatively free to choose the moments of climax. Apparatus, however, often dictates not only the accelerations and decelerations but also the placing of accents.

Once the attention is drawn to the climax within a single action, or the most important action within a series, then the preparation for this moment and the ultimate recovery need to be considered. If the main action is to be effective then both preparation and recovery must be efficient. When these three phases are recognised the inherent *rhythms* within any sequence of movement can be studied, played with and enjoyed. It is important to realise that rhythm should develop naturally from the use of speed and energy appropriate to the action or sequence being performed. It should also be noted that although an increase in speed is usually associated with an increase in the output of energy this need not necessarily be so. Great strength and a considerable amount of energy are required in moving slowly into a difficult balance.

A rhythm can be established by repeating a single action which includes a time change. The rhythm can remain constant or can rhythmically accelerate or decelerate. Rhythm can also be stressed when performing two actions several times, or by accenting the rhythmical timing within a sequence of varied movements.

Having dealt not only with *what* the body does but also *how* an action is performed, elementary movement ideas can be considered anew but with a different stress. The ability to control the speed at which the body moves can be investigated, *e.g.* in the themes of twisting and turning, and flight.

If the time changes naturally associated with producing and releasing torsion are explored, it will be found that two possibilities present themselves. If a complete twist is to be experienced then the body is usually led slowly into position, the speed decreasing as the action reaches its limit and the new base prepared. The release may be quick and explosive if the original base is completely freed, or resolved slowly if contact with the floor is maintained so that weight is taken on both the original and the new base. In the former instance little or no resistance to the unwinding process is possible whereas in the latter the release can be regulated and control over the speed retained. It will be appreciated, however, that these are not the only connections between twisting and time changes, and the more able the performer the more versatile will be his used of speed.

The inherent speeds involved in flight will already have been discovered when dealing with this theme in an elementary way. It is only when sufficient experience and confidence have been acquired, however, that the performer is able to select the appropriate and therefore the most effective blending of speed and energy in order to accomplish a particular objective. Before the more advanced aspects of flight can be attempted the individual should be able to produce and use the speed gathered in take-off and to control the speed on landing. To revise the earlier work on flight, but now with a time stress, produces an ideal link between the elementary and the advanced aspects of the theme.

Before the advanced theme of gaining, maintaining and losing balance is introduced, it is most important to have acquired the physical discipline involved in controlling the speed of the body. The instinctive way of gaining balance is to do so with a decrease of speed as the balance point is reached and the natural reaction to loss of equilibrium is for the body to gain speed. Although this use of time change, stressing deceleration and acceleration, is characteristic of the beginner, the skilled performer can equally well arrive quickly in a balanced position and check the speed at the precise moment of achieving balance. The more able and the more confident he is the greater the "play" will be when losing balance. A deliberate throwing of oneself off balance and catching the weight again, during floor work, on apparatus or in the air, requires skill, courage and a great deal of self assurance. True loss of balance can never be accomplished slowly but the more proficient the gymnast the more versatile he will be in lowering himself out of a balance, restraining his body against the pull of gravity.

The effect on most classes of moving quickly and slowly is easily recognisable and the teacher utilises this knowledge both at the beginning and end of a gymnastic lesson. Quick actions enliven, stimulate and animate, which is one requirement of limbering. The consequence of slower movement is to quieten, calm and relax, the aim at the conclusion of a lesson. Although the class will already be used to the different time stress between the introduction and completion, once speed has been thoroughly explored a greater awareness and variety should become evident in the selection of limbering and calming activities.

If, through gymnastic teaching, it is hoped to foster real competence in movement, then, having first learnt to manage the body in varying situations, mastering the rate at which the body moves should follow logically. This is a facility which must be acquired if the individual is to become expert in the timing of his actions and in the selection of the most expedient use of the skill he has gained.

## Teaching

Most Juniors attack physical tasks with great energy and vigour. This is natural, as slow movements require much greater co-ordination and control, which children of this age have not yet acquired. It has also previously been noted that the young are not concerned with restrained actions neither do they need to consider economy of effort. On the whole they are anxious to accomplish tasks in the minimum amount of time. They are, however, content to repeat an action or series of actions many times, but the speed at which they perform rarely alters. Girls, earlier than boys, become interested in slower, more precise and stylish action, although boys have the greater strength required in order to control the body weight in some of the more difficult slow movements.

With the seven or eight year olds one would not want to inhibit or repress their natural zest and attack in dealing with objective tasks. As they gradually learn to manage their bodies, however, they become more skilful, more co-ordinated and ready to tackle the task of learning to move using a greater variety of time changes. Similarly when Secondary classes have experienced some of the elementary body management skills they can be introduced to tasks concerned with speed. This can come at the beginning of the second year or can be tackled earlier if the teacher assesses it as a need of a particular class.

As with other themes, the extremes should be experienced first, and in this case they will involve the individual moving as slowly or as quickly as he can. Each child must be left quite free to choose his own actions if he is to experiment with confidence. The actions selected must be those he feels he is capable of performing safely at the chosen speed.

The range within the class will be great at first, as each child's interpretation of quick and slow varies. With the help of the teacher and through observation of others, the individual will quickly realise that he is able to extend his own scope of movement within the task. Exploring the extremes of speed should not be pursued to any great degree at this stage. Before progressing further the class should be made aware that actions involving flight are necessarily quick, whereas movements leading into a balance position, although not necessarily so, are relatively slower, while other actions can be performed equally well using either speed.

The first progression is when the children begin to experience the change from one speed to another and build sequences where a time change is evident. Free choice of action and speed preference should still be allowed but the teacher must check that in each case both quick and slow actions are included. For some children their sequence will consist of all quick movements with perhaps only one slow movement apparent, whereas for others the reverse will be so; some will always place the "odd" action at the beginning or end of the sequence.

When the teacher feels that the class is ready to accept imposed speeds he can begin to dictate the rate at which the class must work and where the time changes are to be placed. The choice of action still remains with the individual. The task may be to:

(a) invent a sequence where the stress is on moving slowly, but the first and last actions are quick, or
(b) compose a sequence, alternate actions being quick and slow.

The next stage could be for the teacher to select a simple action which every child is capable of performing, such as a roll, and to give the following challenges:

(c) Choose any roll and repeat it several times bringing about either an increase or decrease in speed.

(d) Within a single rolling action bring about a specific time change, *e.g.* begin quickly losing speed or begin slowly gathering speed.

The class could then be left free to choose other actions and experiment with them in a similar way. It is here the teacher must see that each child selects actions relative to his ability, ensuring that everyone works at his own level. Actions involving inversion, particularly those where weight is taken on the hands, should be included by most. The more skilful the child the greater should be his range of speed, and the more able he should become at performing the same skill quickly and slowly or at the speed necessitated by circumstances. A handstand when performed by a beginner, for example, usually consists of a quick lowering of the upper half of the body and a vigorous upward kick of the legs. The less able the child the less control he can exert over the returning action of the body into the standing position. The more expert performer can complete the action slowly lowering the body into and out of the balance position. This requires great strength, much control and co-ordination. Fine timing and judgment in the use of the two extremes of speed are essential before agilities are attempted which involve a quick swing of the legs as in headsprings and backsprings.

If a time change within a single action is explored and the resulting movement repeated a rhythm can easily be recognised. The child can be made aware of his own individual rhythm and allowed to explore this for himself. By observation he can also appreciate the different rhythms established by others who may even have chosen an identical action.

Junior classes at this stage probably will have reached the limit of their ability and interest in this particular movement idea, and this will possibly be true also of Secondary children in their second year.

Older classes find the more advanced aspects of speed most interesting, and a link can easily be established when working with a partner. Just as new timing has to be experienced when working in twos, so rhythms can be copied, not necessarily matching actions but abstracting the time pattern and reproducing the essential stresses either within an action or sequence. Further individual work on rhythms can now be explored and accelerating and decelerating rhythms attempted. A sequence of movements can be invented and the intrinsic time stresses observed. Climaxes will emerge and natural pauses become obvious. If the sequence is repeated, keeping in mind these discoveries, a greater clarity can be accomplished and the series of actions logically unified.

Attention should be drawn to the fine timing involved in the efficient use of springboards and trampettes, and in dealing with mobile apparatus, if the use of speed is to be employed to advantage. These skills are dealt with in detail in Chapters 12 and 13.

Not only can children be helped to appreciate that the body is capable of moving at varying speeds but also their attention should be drawn to the economical use of speed when performing a physical task. They should also be able to select appropriately the speed required to perform any task efficiently. If children acquire the physical ability to move at a great variety of speeds and are able to select from this variety purposefully, they are in a position to apply this knowledge and ability not only in the gymnasium but in related situations where efficiency and economy of effort are required.

## *Apparatus*

Before planning apparatus for work on this theme several principles should be established. The first is that the apparatus itself can do much to dictate the timing of actions. Inclined forms, spring boards, trampettes, swinging ropes and other mobile pieces of apparatus, as well as partners, determine to a large extent a specific use of speed.

The task set is another factor to be considered. If apparatus has to be cleared, a high bar to be reached or a box mounted, then the need for acceleration is obvious and the challenge will only be met if the necessary amount of energy and speed is gathered and used efficiently. Organisation also has to be re-considered. If the task involves moving slowly, the teacher must provide sufficient apparatus to cover the eventuality of each child spending a comparatively long time on any one piece. Otherwise a situation will arise where one child is working and the rest of the group waiting. If a task to include a time change is given and two pieces of apparatus are provided, *e.g.* a form and a horse, this may also result in queues forming. "A" may choose to move slowly along the form and quickly over the horse, while "B" decides to do the reverse. The teacher here has two alternatives. He may set a more specific challenge, *e.g.* the first attempt of each child must show quick actions along the form and a slow movement over the horse, followed by the reverse. Secondly, he may be able to provide two forms where two children can work at once and adapt to each other if they meet on the horse.

The provision of apparatus to enable a number of children to experiment with changing speed must be prepared with thought and care. If one speed only is to be experienced then a single piece of apparatus will suffice. When asking children to produce a time change, however, a series of actions will probably result. If faced with this task and expected to work on one piece of apparatus such as a horse, buck or box, children are immediately limited either to using the apparatus once or leaving and returning to it. The disadvantages are obvious when considering that there will be perhaps five or six in the group. Long pieces of apparatus such as forms or mattresses which allow for several actions to follow each other easily are preferable. Similarly ropes and bars, which allow three or four to work at once with no hindrance to others, offer greater freedom. A further alternative is to provide a variety of apparatus where children will have sufficient opportunity for moving freely, experiencing the full scope of possibilities within the task.

It is valuable when beginning apparatus work with a Junior class to give them experience of moving consistently at one speed. This stage need not be prolonged but will give the class time to gain confidence in moving quickly and slowly on or over narrow surfaces and at varying levels. The height of apparatus should be kept comparatively low in the first few lessons and, where possible, raised gradually as the children become more experienced. Only single pieces of apparatus are required at this stage and in the Junior school forms, individual or large mats, canes or hoops raised on skittles, steps and bars can be used with the tasks of moving quickly and:

(a) going over or under,
(b) getting on and off,
(c) travelling up, down or along, and
(d) going from side to side.

The first progression for Juniors and a possible way of introducing apparatus work on this theme at Secondary level is to give challenges which direct the attention towards experiencing the extremes of speed, e.g.:

Apparatus—forms.

Task.—Run and jump off the form, land and work away moving slowly.

These two actions could be repeated travelling the length of the form.

Apparatus—a form used broadways so that three children work at once.

*Task.*—Approach and cross the form quickly and return over the form moving slowly.

**Apparatus**—spring board and mattress.

*Task* 1.—Run and jump off the spring board, land and roll over the mat, turn and recross the mat moving slowly. N.B. The teacher can help the class to appreciate that if they return alternately to the right and left, no one need feel hurried by another following too quickly.

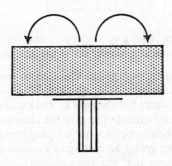

*Task* 2.—Run and jump off the spring board, attempt to check speed immediately on landing and roll slowly across the mat. Own choice of action and speed to return.

**Apparatus**—bar (hip height).

*Task* 1.—Cross over quickly and recross slowly.

*Task* 2.—Progress along the bar, getting over slowly and under quickly.

**Apparatus**—ropes and mats.

*Task* 1.—Run and swing on one or two ropes, jump off, land and roll across the mat.

*Task* 2.—Progressions would be to include a twist or turn at the end of the swing, necessitating a quick action, and for the swing to be repeated several times.

or

Added impetus could be gained at the point when the feet are able to contact the floor and recharge the swing.

or

The challenge of checking the speed on landing, and crossing the mat slowly, could be given.

**Apparatus**—box top and mats. Arrows denote possible starting points.

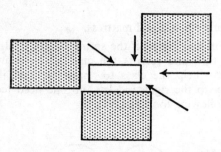

*Task.*—Approach from any angle, run and jump onto and off or over the box quickly, slowly cross the mat nearest on landing.

The teacher should encourage the children to use the free mats on landing and to follow each other quickly. This will not only enliven their awareness of others but the pace of work will not be interrupted. This challenge can be extended to give the class experience in adapting the speed of their actions with no predetermined ideas, fitting in with others in the group according to circumstances. The teacher must, however, ensure that the arrangement includes opportunities for a variety of approach and passing points as shown below.

**Apparatus**—form inclined to a bar box, and a spring board; form leading up to a horse and mat.

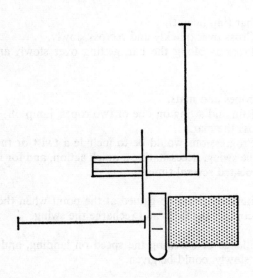

*Task.*—The whole group to work at the same time, individuals to move over the apparatus, adjusting to others as the situation demands.

This task involves a heightened awareness of others working and requires adaptation both of action and timing, so a link could be made here with group work—*see* Chapter 13.

Eventually the gradations between the extremes of speed and the natural accelerations and decelerations necessary when using apparatus will become apparent. The class need to be made aware of these possibilities by a careful selection of apparatus as in the following examples.

**Apparatus**—three inclined forms to the lower of two bars, heights approximately 6 and 16.

*Task.*—Run up the form, pause, turn and run down. N.B. The children should all be able to discover for themselves the natural acceleration and deceleration which occurs in answering this task. They could then alter the action but maintain the increase and decrease in speed, using the top bar to link the accelerating and decelerating actions.

**Apparatus**—ropes, two bars, height to be fixed according to the ability of the majority of the group.

*Task.*—Using one or two ropes, swing on to and grip either both or the higher bar. Get off with an increase or decrease of speed.

**Apparatus**—forms leading up to ropes and mattress.

*Task.*—Run along the form and leap for the rope, swing and land near to the mat and roll across it. The necessity for acceleration on to the rope will be obvious but the teacher could help individuals to recognise the possibilities of deceleration in the roll across the mat. N.B. The distance between the end of each form and the rope can vary according to the ability of individuals and the forms may be altered during the experimental period.

With older forms in the Secondary school who are working on the advanced aspects of this theme, establishing and repeating a rhythm on apparatus can be both exciting and exacting. Using apparatus such as forms, ropes and bars, a rhythm can be evolved in answer to a specific action task, *e.g.* using a single bar, the task could be to get over and under. Using one or two ropes a rhythmical swinging action can easily be achieved or the natural rhythm within a series of actions explored. This sequence could include the use of the floor to approach, an action on the rope, and a means of travelling away from it.

Once children have experienced a regular rhythm using the same piece of apparatus, they can quickly recognise the possibilities of maintaining this rhythm while accelerating or decelerating using more than one piece. The choice and placement of such apparatus can help considerably when working on this aspect of speed. The apparatus selected must either be two or more like pieces, or apparatus with similar dimensions or proportions such as the saddle and horse, the broadside of a form and a box top, or a spring board and trampette.

Most apparatus is adjustable and in the majority of cases the distance between pieces of apparatus can differ and the height at which it is fixed can vary. When introducing accelerating or decelerating rhythms to a class it will probably be most helpful if the first variation of apparatus occurs in height, as for example:

(a) one form, two forms and three forms high (N.B. One child will be required to steady the two forms and two to stabilise the three),

(b) one form, a box top and two layers of the box,

(c) a saddle on a low bar, another on a higher bar and the horse,

(d) a beating board or form, a spring board and trampette.

The teacher must ensure that the starting points vary, either beginning with the apparatus which is lowest or the highest, so that not only acceleration but also deceleration is experienced.

Having explored these possibilities the need to increase the distance between apparatus in order to negotiate the increase in height will probably be observed and alterations can be made accordingly.

Some fixed apparatus such as the window ladders, wall bars and ropes, unlike the bars, cannot be adjusted. The ropes, however, are mobile and the size of the swing can vary, therefore an individual could invent a rhythmical sequence and using each rope in turn gradually increase or decrease the amount of speed and energy used.

On window ladders or frames which produce gaps of equal dimensions, rhythmical actions could be performed and repeated, increasing or decreasing speed and travelling up, down, diagonally or across.

It is realised that this aspect of speed uses space and apparatus extravagantly, but if the teacher realises the possibilities he may decide to include perhaps one or two of the above ideas in his general apparatus plan. With an able class who have fully explored accelerating, decelerating and simple rhythms the teacher might feel justified, when planning apparatus, in covering all aspects of this last idea at once. The task for all would be to experiment with accelerating and decelerating rhythms, and the apparatus selected from the following:

(*a*) a set of ropes;

(*b*) window ladders or frame or wall bars;

(*c*) one form, one box top and two layers of the box, or one form, two layers of the box and a buck;

(*d*) beating board, spring board and trampette;

(*e*) two or three bars, if possible, at different heights;

(*f*) one form, two forms and three forms;

(*g*) one saddle on the floor, one on a low beam and a horse. N.B. If weight is to be taken on the hands on the first saddle, then the teacher must ensure that two children are used to steady the apparatus at either side, but this is not necessary if the apparatus is used for rolling over or sliding through;

(*h*) a horse, between a saddle on a low bar and one on a higher bar;

(*i*) on the Cave Southampton apparatus saddles could be fixed to bars arranged at three different heights.

A further consideration of this theme occurs when timing and judgment of moving apparatus become necessary. Travelling to make eventual contact with a swinging rope, for example, involves judging the speed of the oncoming rope and timing the action of gripping so finely that no interruption occurs in the process. The following tasks could be given to provide children with initial experience.

**Apparatus**—ropes, trapeze or rings.

*Task* 1.—Hold the rope and swing it away; as it returns, time the moment of contact, grip, and travel on it. The individual can experiment with contacting the rope at different stages of the swing.

*Task* 2.—A similar task can be given using trapeze or rings.

**Apparatus**—form and ropes.

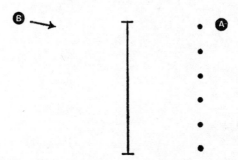

*Task* 1.—In twos—A swings the rope to B—B runs and jumps off the form to swing on the rope.

*Task* 2.—Repeat the challenge of Task 2 but land back on the form. This is a progression and involves timing in judgment of not only when to grip but also when to release.

**Apparatus**—two forms and ropes.

*Task.*—Set all ropes swinging. Cross and recross from one form to another using each rope in turn and travel along a zigzag path.

**Apparatus**—trampette and trapeze.

*Task.*—Run and use the trampette to contact and swing on the trapeze, which has previously been set in motion. A progression would be to land back on the trampette from the trapeze or to arrive on a piece of apparatus placed on the other side of the trapeze.

An extension of this idea can be incorporated into an aerial circuit where trapeze, rings and ropes can be used in conjunction with trampettes and other pieces of portable apparatus to provide a most challenging arrangement.

Accents and climax within a sequence of actions can readily be recognised and stressed once the class has experienced accelerations, decelerations and rhythms. Appreciation of appropriate actions to stress or highlight can add clarity and enliven the work on apparatus, but the teacher must always be aware of unnecessary or illogical emphasis.

PLATES 14–17.—Examples of obstacles being negotiated with contrasting body shapes

Plate 14

Plate 15

Plate 16

Plate 17

# CHAPTER 8

# CONTINUITY OF MOVEMENT IN ACTION

## *Material*

CONTINUITY is a state where movements follow each other in succession, so interwoven that one arises as a natural outcome of the previous action. This does not presuppose that the body must sustain a continuous state of motion. Active pauses which occur as a necessary preparation or involve balance can all be part of an integrated sequence.

In gymnastics there is still a need to perform a single skill in isolation. The emphasis, however, is on the added ability required to combine a variety of actions, relevant to the task set, and so linked that the sequence is a logical whole. A sequence is a series of bodily actions where recovery and preparation of each action are so skilfully linked and movement so fluent that actual phases are indistinguishable except in variations of rhythm. Economy of effort becomes increasingly important once a number of movements are required. The initial momentum can often be utilised in following actions and the natural use of body weight can be exploited.

All actions are preceded by a preparation and followed by a recovery. The preparatory stage may be brief or comparatively long; the recovery may be quick or take time, and in single actions both can usually be distinguished easily. Within a series, however, it is possible for the recovery and preparation to overlap and it is this blending that brings about continuity.

In gymnastics once movements become deliberate and selected it is not merely a physical preparation and recovery that is considered; mentally the performer has to be alert, anticipating ways of leading naturally into the next action. Those children who are skilled and versatile have a greater choice of action and are therefore more likely to achieve continuity than those who have mastered only one way of leading into and out of a particular skill. Previous work on achieving a variety of preparations for and recoveries from a specific skill proves of added value when continuity has to be considered.

If movements are to be linked smoothly with no irregular interruption occurring within a sequence, the performer must be aware of transitional actions and the part or parts of the body which are about to receive weight. These parts must be prepared in the recovery of the previous action so that on contact with the floor or apparatus

I                              115

the placement affords a sufficiently stable base on to or over which the body may move.

The way in which the body arrives over the base is important. Weight may be transferred on to the new part with a wave-like action involving successive arrival or with the body arriving simultaneously, using an action in which all parts are affected concurrently. Successive arrivals lead more easily to continuous movements; in simultaneous arrivals the action has normally to be recharged before continuing. Reference can be made to other themes, *e.g.* twisting and turning, and loss of balance, where continuity is a natural outcome.

## Teaching

Continuity is the thread which runs throughout all other gymnastic themes and is a facet of the work to which teachers should constantly refer.

Beginners find difficulty in linking unlike movements smoothly, although the same action can often be repeated several times. Dissimilar actions which are simple and involve weight transference from feet to feet only, can more easily be joined, as in running and bouncing, hopping and leaping. A greater skill is demanded when linking actions which include weight transference on to a variety of bases, particularly when inversion takes place and where change of direction and variation of level occur.

A progressive set of tasks could be as follows, each being developed as the teacher deems necessary.

*Task 1.*—Bounce along using two feet together.

*Task 2.*—Travel leaping from one foot to the other.

*Task 3.*—Run and jump, repeat several times.

*Task 4.*—Transfer weight from feet to hands, repeat this action travelling.

*Task 5.*—Run and jump, on landing add an action which keeps the body near to the ground.

*Task 6.*—Start with weight on feet, body tucked, roll in any direction and jump up again. Repeat several times and then change the direction of the roll.

*Task 7.*—Practice No. 5 with turns in the air.

*Task 8.*—Take weight on to the hands, get one or both feet high into the air and on landing roll.

*Task 9.*—Start with weight on feet, body tucked, and roll in any direction. Transfer weight on to hands, back on to feet and end with a jump.

In the early stages the teacher must ensure that the children realise the need to think ahead. This readiness and anticipation should be encouraged and the first steps taken in learning how to land in a position which leads easily into the next movement. This will involve a deliberate selection of part or parts to receive weight and preparation of others required to initiate the following movement. The appropriate speed at which to work must also be considered.

*Example.*—If a handstand is to be preceded by a forward roll, most children will have to consider how to lead into the inversion. This will usually be by swinging one leg into the air and pushing with the other. At the end of the roll, therefore, the feet should be placed one in front of the other so that they can be used as needed. The speed of the roll must be such that the forward momentum gathered allows the weight to be transferred straight on to the hands without readjustment.

Specific practice could be given at this stage in linking skills:

*Task 1.*—perform either a forward or backward roll and
  (*a*) walk out of the action,
  (*b*) jump out of the action,
  (*c*) immediately transfer weight on to the hands, getting hips high.

*Task 2.*—choose an inverted position and
  (*a*) roll out of the inversion,
  (*b*) roll into the inversion,
  (*c*) tip or twist out of the inversion.

At first the stress will be on achieving fluency within a sequence, sustaining continuous movement. The teacher should soon be able to help the class appreciate that pauses are not synonymous with stopping. A change of direction, for example, often requires a hesitation as the point is reached when control of momentum is such that redirection of the body weight becomes possible. Children can experience this quite simply in rocking and rolling on to the feet bringing about a change of direction.

Once the more advanced situations of working with others have been explored, sequences can be developed to stress continuity. In a partner sequence where each alternately provides and clears the obstacle, the added challenge of linking actions can be a demanding one.

So far continuity has been brought about by a prior selection of actions. The more skilled the individual the more easily he can invent a phrase of movement spontaneously. This, however, involves a facility to recognise and adapt actions relative to each other as they occur. Often Juniors can be observed acting first and then thinking, while Secondary children tend to think first before moving. The spontaneous reaction of Juniors should not be lost and the thought applied to movement at Secondary level must also be encouraged. The ability to "think bodily" should be fostered, as a fusion of action and thought is one of the main aims in teaching gymnastics.

### Apparatus

On apparatus this theme should rarely be taken in isolation for more than two or three consecutive lessons. It is an underlying consideration in all apparatus work and will often be referred to and drawn upon as a subsidiary idea. Once the class, group or individual, for example, has mastered a particular movement challenge, this can then be developed to include continuity of action. If the teacher observes that a class shows a lack of ability or appreciation in this respect, specific tasks can be given to help.

It is, however, a movement idea that could be used successfully to introduce the work to Secondary classes who have been trained formally, and in this case more time could be devoted to it. Skills already mastered can be included, giving a degree of security, while the added task of joining actions can be readily grasped and easily observed.

In selecting apparatus for continuity tasks the teacher should ensure that the difference between levels is not too great at first. A form leading up to a high box, for example, rarely helps the beginner maintain continuous actions, but a form leading up to three layers of the box, or a form inclined on to a bar box, is a more helpful arrangement.

Placing apparatus in a straight line will also facilitate an uninterrupted series of actions, whereas having to manage apparatus placed at right angles tends to hamper all but the most able at first.

Tasks which stress resiliency and where the apparatus is duplicated or is long enough for actions to be repeated, help to ensure that continuity is gained. For example:

1. A form or bar used lengthways.
2. Two forms with mats placed between and used broadways.

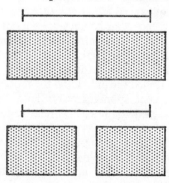

3. A bar with three saddles placed at regular intervals.
4. Two low box tops and mats.

Different ways of landing on apparatus can be explored and the teacher could point out that landing on hands and knees on the box top, for example, is a difficult position from which to move with any degree of continuity. If the landing, however, is on to one or both feet, or hands and feet, the next action is comparatively easy to initiate. It is often after arriving on apparatus that adjustment has to be made and the following tasks could be given to help children in this respect. During the experimental period the teacher could refer to successive and simultaneous arrivals on the apparatus.

**Apparatus**—box (two layers).

 *Task* 1.—Run and spring on to the box on one foot, step on to the other and push into a jump, land and roll.
 *Task* 2.—Run and arrive on hands and feet, make the landing of the feet the preparation to push off again, hands remaining on the box until the feet have landed.
 *Task* 3.—Arrive on two hands and one foot, use the free leg to initiate the movement off.

**Apparatus**—ropes and horse or box or buck.

 *Task* 1.—Use one or two ropes to land on the apparatus. Practise arriving on different body parts, *e.g.* one or two feet, hips, one knee.
 *Task* 2.—Use the ropes as above, land on one part and from this position use the free parts of the body to initiate the next action.

The ease and fluency with which actions are performed and linked on apparatus are the hallmarks of the advanced gymnast. It is only the most skilled performer who reaches the point where movements merge so naturally that the sequence assumes a logicality and completeness, simple for the observer to appreciate but most difficult to attain.

# CHAPTER 9

# PARTNER WORK

To work with another person is not a new idea in gymnastics; in the formal approach partners assisted each other and balances and vaults were often achieved by one helping the other. This way of working together is still of value, but from it new aspects of partner work have developed, for not only can one help another but both can work together with an equal stress.

Partner work is not merely a means of repeating the basic skills with another person, but in itself can be challenging, exciting and rewarding. In any situation where two people work together there is bound to be a certain amount of "give and take" and this is true in the gymnastic sense. The pair learn, to a greater or lesser degree, to share ideas and select from them appropriately. Sometimes a situation is reached in which one partner must learn a new skill and then the pair have to decide if this is possible, or, if not, how to re-adjust the sequence.

Working with a partner involves a high degree of accuracy in performance—each action must be repeated exactly, not only in the way that the body is used but also in the timing of the action, and this helps to train movement memory. If one partner is learning an action from the other, the performer has to be consistent in what he does and the observer must be able to understand what he sees. In addition to accurate performance, movement memory and movement observation, other equally important factors have their place in partner work. Working with a partner will always involve experiencing new rhythms and timing. As an individual it is very easy to work on the floor, literally at one's own pace, unless the teacher is aware of this and is able to give specific experience in re-timing bodily actions. When working with another person it is not always possible to use one's habitual timing. It is often necessary to go faster or slower, to accelerate or decelerate in order to match or adapt.

Although all the above aspects of partner work are valuable, the most important factor and the reason for including this type of work in gymnastics, is that in this situation activities can be explored and mastered which are impossible to do alone. The ultimate aim of working with another person is to achieve interdependence and this is a unique situation in gymnastics.

## *Material*

Unlike other gymnastic themes (with the exception of group work), working with a partner is not so much concerned with a movement idea but with the very movement situations arising from two people tackling a common task. It is quite possible to give two children a movement challenge such as travelling, stressing symmetry and asymmetry and for them to answer with a joint sequence. However, this is of limited value.

The fun and point of working with another is in discovering and mastering the situations that arise from doing, sharing and helping. This is not the creative relationship of a dance duo but of two people working objectively together.

There are four basic partner situations:

1. Copying part or whole of a partner's sequence.
2. Making and negotiating obstacles (without contact).
3. Matching actions.
4. Taking all or part of each other's weight.

### 1. COPYING PART OR WHOLE OF A PARTNER'S SEQUENCE

(a) *Following pathways.*—One travels, the other follows, *i.e.* "follow the leader" relationship. Here it is only the pathway that is dictated by the leader "A": the actual way in which "A" travels—running, leaping, rolling—is not copied. "B" chooses his own movement but follows "A's" track.

(b) *Following pathways and copying the main idea.*—As above but "B" now tries to copy the way "A" travels. This is not yet exact copying but "B" uses the same idea as "A"; *e.g.* "A" might travel by cartwheeling, while "B" copies the essence of this, *i.e.* travelling with weight on hands, feet overtaking, in a sideways direction.

(c) *Copying a short, simple sequence.*—In both the above, "A" and "B" have worked simultaneously, or "B" has followed after a short delay, during which he assesses "A's" movement. Now "A" performs a sequence which "B" observes and then tries to copy. "A's" sequence must be clear in action and remain unchanged in repetition; "B," having observed, aims to perform "A's" sequence as accurately as possible.

### 2. MAKING AND NEGOTIATING OBSTACLES (WITHOUT CONTACT)

(a) *Basic body-shapes forming obstacles.*—"A" makes a body shape suggested by the teacher, *e.g.* a curled shape which "B" goes over.

(b) *Changing base and angle of approach.*—"A" changes the base, *i.e.* takes weight on different parts of the body, but maintains a curled shape. "B" goes over as before but begins to vary the angle of approach.

(*c*) *Changing shape and way of negotiating.*—The teacher continues to give ideas of the shape that the obstacle could take, *e.g.* wide or arched, and suggests how "B" negotiates this, *i.e.* under or through.

(*d*) *Choice of negotiation according to shape presented.*—"A" selects and makes a body shape which "B" has to negotiate appropriately, *e.g.* by sliding under a low bridge shape; "A" changes his shape and "B" chooses whether to go over, under or through, and how to do this. "B's" choice of action should be relevant to the obstacle made by "A."

(*e*) *Continuous interchanging.*—Although each child has worked as "A" and "B" it has been in the nature of having turns at providing the obstacles and taking turns at negotiating. Now it should be possible for "A" and "B" to interchange, *e.g.* "A" makes a shape which "B" goes over, immediately making a different shape for "A."

(*f*) *Interchanging with split-second timing.*—As a further development, fine timing could be stressed, *e.g.* "A" rolls into a shoulder stand with legs apart just before "B" goes through this gap and into a movement which leads to a curled position on the floor ready for "A" to leap over.

(*g*) *Moving obstacles.*—The most demanding aspect of partners providing obstacles for each other is when the obstacle itself is moving. In this "A" and "B" would both be moving throughout the sequence, each in turn providing or going over the obstacle.

### 3. MATCHING ACTIONS

This involves the pair doing exactly the same actions at the same time, or one after the other. The starting positions indicate the possibilities with this idea.

(*a*) *Side by side facing the same direction.*—This is probably the simplest way because the starting situation can be maintained throughout the sequence and the performers can see each other whilst working.

(*b*) *Side by side facing different directions.*—Here A and B will work away from, towards or will pass each other and will sometimes be in situations where they are unable to maintain a visual contact.

(*c*) *Facing each other with a mirror-like relationship.*—*i.e.* "A" moves to his right, "B" moves to his left.

(*d*) *Facing each other with a non-mirror-like relationship.*—*i.e.* "A" moves to his right while "B" moves to his right. This would involve moving towards and away from each other.

(*e*) *Back to back.*—This also brings about moving away and towards the partner but because the two cannot see each other the problem of exact timing becomes very difficult.

(*f*) *One behind the other facing the same direction.*—The couple can move together but are in a good position to exploit the possibility of moving in canon.

## 4. TAKING ALL OR PART OF EACH OTHER'S WEIGHT

(*a*) *"A" helps "B" to achieve and maintain a balance.*—This should be a balance which "B" finds difficult or impossible to do alone.

(*b*) *"B" gets over "A" or pushes off "A" to gain flight.*—By means of a brief contact "B" uses "A" to achieve flight; a well known example of this is leap-frog but there are many other possibilities.

(*c*) *Balancing on a partner.*—Having had experience of momentarily taking each other's weight, the children should be introduced to more skilled aspects of working together. "A" selects a position in which he is stable and "B" balances on "A," *i.e.* "B's" weight is taken and held by "A" and "B" is dependent upon "A" to provide a steady base.

The above ways of taking all or part of each other's weight involve one partner acting as a piece of apparatus, solid, firm and unyielding. In the following examples both children are active, continuously concerned with the problems of adjusting and readjusting to each other's weight or timing. This may be seen clearly by comparing (*b*) with (*f*). In each case "B" achieves flight but in the first situation "A's" role is almost entirely passive, whereas in the second both "A" and "B" are active. There are many ways in which the interdependence of the pair can be developed.

(*d*) *Gaining, holding and losing balance on a partner.*—A progression is when the support "A" is able to adjust his position to help "B" achieve and maintain the balance and then by re-adjustment of his body is able to tip "B" so that at a pre-determined moment balance is lost. Many interesting and difficult balances can be invented once the pair realise that parts of the body can be used to grip.

(*e*) *Lifting, carrying and lowering.*—Situations involving one lifting, carrying and lowering the other can be explored and these demand great skill.

(*f*) *Working in twos to achieve flight.*—Another skilled aspect of this type of partner work is when "A" helps "B" to achieve flight. "A" may assist "B's" take-off by adding to his ejecting powers, "A" can also help "B" to maintain flight—this would come into the category of assisted flight—and finally "A" can help "B" to make a safe, controlled landing. It is possible, therefore, for "A" to aid "B" in all the three phases of flight or to assist with only one or two.

(*g*) *Counter-balance and counter-tension.*—Perhaps the most diffi-cult way in which two people can work together is when movements involving counter-balance and counter-tension are stressed.

*Counter-balance*—By pushing against or "propping up" and making adjustments in the area of their common base and in the angle of leaning, a position is achieved in which both are inter-dependent, each providing a force which balances and offsets the other. Having established positions of counter-balance, the pair may then travel, rotate, raise and lower themselves, their actions being towards their common centre and their common base re-maining wide.

*Counter-tension*—By gripping each other, their common base remaining small, and pulling or leaning away, a balance position is felt when the body is subjected to forces acting in opposite direc-tions, *i.e.* the pull of the partner through the gripping limbs and the pull of the rest of the body, which leans away from both partner and base. A couple can experience many different counter-tensions by using a variety of grips and bases and exploiting the asym-metrical possibilities of the body.

Once positions of counter-balance and counter-tension have been experienced it is profitable for the pair to investigate ways of coming together to achieve them, and to discover what happens if, from such positions, one of the pair exerts a stronger force than the other or contact is broken.

## Teaching

Before introducing partner work the children should have had considerable experience in managing the body and also be competent in the handling of apparatus. The latter is vital because working with someone else often necessitates handling, gripping, lifting and lower-ing, and unless previous experience in manœuvring apparatus is given children cannot be expected to work together safely and pro-fitably.

The introductory stages of partner work could be taken in the last two years of the Junior School and with a very able class, whose movement experience is wide, it should be possible to go much further. In the Secondary School it is difficult to say at what stage such material should be introduced because the previous movement training of the children varies so much. Ideally, the partner work begun in the Junior School should be developed but more often than not the first year has to be spent in gaining elementary skill and an understanding of movement, and it is not until later, probably in the second year, that partner work can be introduced.

Once children have become familiar with the partner situation it is of value to keep referring to it in subsequent work. Instead of teaching the theme with all its progressions in one year, the more demanding work should be kept until individuals gain in skill and powers of invention.

It is important that the teacher is aware that in introducing partner work he is putting the child in a completely new movement situation. Previously each child has had to consider his classmates in various circumstances. When working on the floor he has learnt how to change direction or twist out of the way to avoid collisions, he has moved large pieces of apparatus with the help of others, and in working on apparatus he is accustomed to taking his turn and sharing. Now, for the first time, the stress is not on looking after oneself or fitting in with a group but on a partnership, on working wholly with one other person. Because this is a new situation it is essential that all the introductory stages are given. With Secondary children it may only be necessary to go through these simply and briefly in a few lessons, not stopping to perfect any one aspect but giving them as situations to be explored. However, in the Junior School these stages are invaluable and could be profitably pursued, the partners working at each problem and perfecting a finished sequence.

Once partner work involving following a pathway or copying a series of actions is introduced, the progressions are varied and depend upon the movement characteristics of the class. A lively, energetic group who like to get over things and are more concerned with what they do rather than how they do it, would probably enjoy making obstacles for each other. A class with a fine sense of timing would be more interested in partner work where exact matching of both actions and speed is stressed. Having successfully perfected such sequences, each of these classes could be helped to improve its bodily skill and understanding of movement by working at what is, for them, the more difficult aspect of partner work.

The actual choosing of partners is probably best left to the children at first, or the teacher can arrange the twos in approximately the same weight and size, but later, with growing understanding, skill and confidence, opportunities should be given for working with different partners.

## 1. COPYING PART OR WHOLE OF A PARTNER'S SEQUENCE

(a) *Following pathways.*—Here the leader "A" must be helped to realise that it is his track that is important to "B" and so it must be both clear and varied. The direction of the pathway is in relation to the room and will be composed of zigzags, loops, straight lines and circles. The way in which "A" travels (forwards, backwards, sideways) is not copied and is therefore not so important.

(b) *Following pathways and copying the main idea.*—This is a much more difficult task for "B" and the teacher can help in several ways. First, it is important to see that the space in which the two work is limited, otherwise the pathway can become too complicated. If mats are available "A's" track can be confined to approaching, crossing and going round the mat. Secondly, the sequences need to be fairly short, probably not more than three actions; "A" must be encouraged to move with clarity and be able to repeat exactly. Young Juniors would enjoy this task if just one action were repeated, *e.g.* weight on hands and feet alternately on a zigzag track. Older children would be able to recognise and copy more than one action. A typical example would be if "A" ran, jumped, landed and rolled. It would not matter if the take-off was from one or two feet, and neither the position of the body in the air nor the type of roll would be important, "B" would follow "A's" pathway and copy the actions of running, jumping and rolling, *i.e.* travelling on feet, being in the air and finally transferring weight to and from adjacent parts in a rolling action.

(c) *Copying a short, simple sequence.*—It would be of value here if the teacher gave each child sufficient time to perfect his own sequence of actions. The observer's task is made easier if the sequence he is watching is well executed and consistent. The teacher's role in this partner activity depends to a large extent upon his knowledge of the class. The following situations would probably occur in an average class.

*Couple X.*—These are both skilled performers with well developed powers of observation, quite capable of seeing and then copying a sequence, eventually doing it well. Obviously the teacher can afford to leave these two, although the temptation is to spend valuable time helping the most able couples.

*Couple Y.*—Here the two quite quickly copy the essence of each other's sequences but have ignored the subtleties, *e.g.* taking weight entirely on the shoulders is copied as a shoulderstand with the arms propping up the body and therefore taking some of the weight. The teacher needs to help the children to appreciate these discrepancies—it may be that the original sequence was performed in a "slapdash" way, the child being unaware of what his body was doing. It could be that the observation was poor, ignoring detail. The teacher then would help this couple, or the whole class if the problem was a common one, towards a greater awareness in moving, and observing with understanding.

*Couple Z.*—One child finds that he is unable to do one of the actions in his partner's sequence, *e.g.* a balanced headstand. If the teacher thinks that the child is "on the brink" of this particular skill, it would be worth while to help. The ways in which the teacher can help are varied, depending upon the particular difficulty of the child. It may be that encouragement is needed, or that the action needs to be clarified before the child will attempt to copy it. In the latter case the teacher could suggest that while the partner demonstrates the particular action, he and the child will observe together in order to find out how the body is used: "where are the hands placed in relation to the head?" "what is the action of the lower half of the body?" Sometimes it might be necessary for the teacher to give the child support so that he feels what it is like to take and maintain balance on the head and hands and yet is not in danger of falling. With increased confidence and understanding of what he is to do, the child will probably be able to copy his partner's skill without further help from the teacher.

However, if the teacher realises from knowledge of the movement capabilities of the child that he is not at this particular time able to balance on head and hands, he would suggest an action which is as near the original as possible, *i.e.* the body being inverted, though probably not fully stretched, and weight taken on head and hands, be it only for a second.

In answering this task many children will find that it is the timing of the copied sequence that is difficult, rather than the actual movements, and once more it is the teacher who must decide how capable individuals are of achieving an exact copy of both actions and timing. However, it must be stressed that only by constant challenging will individuals widen their movement vocabulary and understanding.

## 2. MAKING AND NEGOTIATING OBSTACLES (WITHOUT CONTACT)

The point of children making obstacles for each other to go over, under, around and through when apparatus has been specifically designed for the purpose could be queried. This query would be valid if a teacher gave this task and did not develop the idea. When seen within the whole context of partner work, however, making and negotiating obstacles become valuable basic training for the more skilled and complex aspects to follow and there is no doubt that children find such problems exciting.

In the elementary task suggested in 2(*a*), p. 121, the children making and negotiating shapes need considerable awareness and sensitivity towards each other, for jumping over a body presents greater problems than scrambling over a box. The child making the curled shape should appreciate the necessity of keeping his body compact, tucking in all angular parts. The child clearing the obstacle must be aware of the importance of judging exactly where to take off, knowing whether height or length is to be stressed in flight, and landing away from his partner. These considerations are obvious and normally children would take such things literally in their stride, but the teacher should stress them from the safety aspect and because such awareness is vital in the later, more difficult partner situations.

In (*b*) and (*c*) the teacher further guides the experience so that the obstacle varies in shape and size and ways of going over, under and through are discovered. The majority of children clearing a small obstacle will run forward and jump over and will want to repeat this several times. Next the teacher could encourage variations: the jump need not always be a forward one, nor from feet to feet; possibilities such as diving over into a roll, cartwheeling over, turning jumps over, rolling under, sliding under, can all be experienced. (*See* Plates 14–18.)

The teacher, therefore, gives or stimulates ideas in (*a*), (*b*) and (*c*) so that by (*d*) the children have sufficient material from which to select for themselves.

In teaching this aspect it is of value with Junior and lower Secondary classes to give the partners ample time to work at and perfect a sequence as suggested in (*d*) and (*e*). It cannot be said too often that although the teacher may give the class a wide movement experience and encourage variety in ideas, unless the children are given an opportunity to develop these ideas, select appropriately from them and eventually perfect their own sequences, little will be added to their movement vocabulary.

The tasks suggested in (*f*) and (*g*) are comparatively difficult but children who are able to accept such challenges will gain much enjoyment and satisfaction from working at these.

It may be necessary with some classes to introduce the idea of coping with a moving obstacle in a simple way first. The following three situations could be given as the starting points upon which each couple would eventually base their own solution to the task set.

*Example* 1.—"A" maintains a rocking action, "B" assesses the moving obstacle, seeing at what point it is best for him to leap over, and at what intervals this opportunity occurs. Although "A" is providing a moving obstacle his actions are predictable, being repetitive, rhythmic, and traversing the same small area.

*Example 2.*—"A" repeats a series of compact rolls in a straight pathway, "B" goes over "A" by means of repetitive jumps making a zigzag pathway. The progression here for "B" is that "A" is travelling in one direction, not crossing and recrossing a given area, and therefore as well as getting over "A," "B" must also travel, either in his actual jump or between jumps.

*Example 3.*—"A" rolls continuously sideways in an elongated position while "B" jumps over "A." Here it is important to note that "B" is faced with two possibilities, either travelling in the same or opposite direction as "A," the latter being the easier. Whether "B" chooses to work towards "A" or travel in the same direction as "A," the actual clearing will demand judgment in the timing and placing of the action.

The teacher will appreciate that when partners are alternately making and negotiating obstacles they are faced with a new situation. In previous work with apparatus, once the pieces have been set up they have not altered in shape or size. In partner work, however, a child can quickly change the shape and outline of his body and vary level, producing a variety of spaces and gaps, so that his partner is constantly having to re-assess the situation confronting him. Similarly, when the obstacle is moving, the challenge is a unique one, none of the conventional apparatus being mobile in this respect.

## 3. MATCHING ACTIONS

Although it may be necessary for each pair to experience all the different starting situations and their influence on the movements that follow, it will be found that if children working in twos are given the problem of matching their movements in various situations, they will generally include more than one way of working together, *e.g.* a sequence which begins side by side may change, because the children roll backwards on opposite shoulders, to one of facing each other.

Any task involving the matching of actions and timing is a demanding one. The pair are not only concerned with doing the same action, *e.g.* rolling, but also performing the action in an identical manner, that is, *what* is done, *how* it is done and *where* are important. (*See* Plate 19.)

Generally, it will be found that children have little difficulty performing the same actions or series of actions. If the short sequence that the pair are doing consists of an asymmetrical shoulder balance which goes into weight being taken on one knee and then into a forward roll, the average couple will be able to do this side by side or facing each other and achieve a certain degree of uniformity. However, once the pair can do the same actions they should be encouraged to aim for exact matching. In the above sequence they would need to know if the weight is taken completely on one shoulder, how the rest of the body maintains the balance and the way in which balance is lost. The arrival on the knee could be preceded by the whole body tipping off balance or by one leg reaching out towards the floor and the knee gradually taking the weight as it is shifted over from the shoulder. The task of moving identically is a considerable challenge to two children and it demands and encourages a heightened sense of body awareness.

Along with the precision of bodily actions the pair must also consider the timing of these actions. Perhaps one of the pair always rolls slowly, coming naturally to a stop as his feet meet the ground, while the other habitually rushes through his roll, gaining impetus. In order to achieve the same rhythm two possibilities are open to the pair. Either child can abandon his own timing of the roll (not an easy thing to do, particularly with a less skilled performer) and attempt to copy that of his partner, or both could work towards each other's timing, resulting in a new way of rolling for both. The moment the pair achieve a common timing can be one of the most exciting and satisfying results of working together.

It is in such situations that the "give and take" of partner work is evident and the teacher must see that this is indeed a shared experience and not allow one of the pair to do all the adapting and adjusting while the other continues to work in his own particular way. The degree of "give and take" both in ideas and performance will vary with each couple, and their relative skill and experience must be taken into account, but ideally the work should be the result of joint contribution.

During the working out of a matching sequence the pair will need considerable time to observe each other and to repeat some actions in isolation, but when the whole movement phrase is being perfected it is useful to link the pairs. One couple watches a nearby couple's sequence and helps them to achieve both matching and synchronisation.

### 4. TAKING ALL OR PART OF EACH OTHER'S WEIGHT

It is important to realise here the development from (2). The basic idea of using the partner as an obstacle remains but contact is now involved. It cannot be stressed too strongly that this is advanced gymnastic work. The teacher is at all times responsible for the safety of the class and it is dangerous to attempt such tasks unless the children are already competent and experienced in handling apparatus. Contact with a partner in order to lift, lower or balance must never be allowed to degenerate into uncontrolled heaving and hauling.

PLATE 18.—Example of obstacle being negotiated using a matching body shape

PLATE 19.—Ten-year-olds matching positions

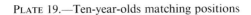

Plate 20

Plate 21

Plate 22

Plate 23

Plate 24

Plate 25

(a) "A" helps "B" to achieve and maintain a balance.—Here the task is for "B" to attempt a balance that he finds difficult, with "A" helping in an appropriate way. If the example of balancing on hands is taken it will be seen that "A" is free to move and take up any position in which he will be able to help "B" gain and maintain balance. Some children will quite happily do a handstand against a wall but not in a space for fear of toppling over, so the helpers think that they can give the security of the wall by catching and holding the legs. This is not only dangerous since the legs are often swung energetically, but usually futile. With a few children who are almost able to do a handstand it may be sufficient for their partners to steady the balance by placing a hand behind the heels. However, with most children it is the trunk, particularly the hips that need to be helped into the vertical position. The helper "A," therefore, should be prepared to give support to those parts that need it and gradually to lessen it as "B" becomes more skilled. The hips or the whole of "B's" trunk can be supported by "A," the latter actually using his body as a wall (See Plate 20) or by gripping and holding other inverted balances (See Plate 21.)

When given the appropriate assistance, "B" actually feels what it is like to be balanced on his hands. He is also made aware of parts that he needs to stabilise, e.g. shoulders and back, by the points at which "A" is giving him support. In addition, the way in which "A" is helping (holding the hips vertically over the base, stopping the legs going past the point of balance) will indicate where he needs to use more or less energy. If "B" is eventually to be able to take weight and balance upon his hands unaided, "A" must be a sympathetic helper. He must appreciate where and when to give support and how this can be gradually decreased, and through observation he must be able to adjust and adapt his support to "B's"changing needs. If "A" himself has the particular skill that "B" is trying to master, it could be an advantage, but this is not necessarily so.

The task of one helping the other to achieve a difficult balance can be made more demanding for the able performer if it is suggested that the base can be distributed upon two levels. Thus one hand could be placed on the floor and the other on the partner's knee as shown in Plate 22.

It should be possible by sympathetic help and guidance from the teacher for children to help each other to acquire balancing skills, although in cases where there is a particular difficulty the teacher may feel that he himself must act as the helper "A."

Problems of balancing the body on bases other than the feet, and particularly in the inverted position, are important in gymnastics and partner work is one way in which the children can become familiar with these situations. Once confidence and mastery have been gained

K

children should normally be able to progress from being helped to working alone on the floor and on apparatus. This, therefore, is an aspect of partner work where the final aim is not of interdependence but where by working together one is helped to become self-sufficient.

(b) *"B" gets over "A" or pushes off "A" to gain flight.*—The brief contact here between the two needs careful consideration. The child acting as the obstacle must take up a position with a wide, stable base and be able to resist the push of his partner as he goes over or around. This means that "A's" body must be firm and parts such as the shoulders which might give way under pressure must be stabilised, as in the familiar leap-frog "back" position, by placing the hands on the knees or thighs. It is also important that "A" knows from what direction the push will come and where contact will be made. If "B" is going over "A" to achieve flight to the side or to go around, the pressure will come from that side at an oblique angle and this will necessitate "A" readjusting his base.

The point of contact between the two needs attention because both must realise that certain parts of "A's" body, *e.g.* the small of the back, are not able to withstand vigorous pushing actions, while other areas, such as the hips, can offer more resistance.

(c) *Balancing on a partner.*—Once the pair are able to cope with temporary contact they are ready to try out situations in which contact is maintained, and the task of "B" balancing on "A" is one way of experiencing this. Again it is necessary for "A's" position to be a stable one with a base sufficiently wide to be able to withstand the extra weight of "B," and the problem of choosing suitable parts of "A's" trunk and limbs upon which to balance has still to be considered. With "B's" weight being borne entirely by "A" it is essential that the latter is helped to select positions in which he can do this safely and effectively, and "B" must help by keeping a light tension throughout his body, that is, endeavouring to control his weight rather than becoming a dead weight draped over "A."

Although this task is ultimately concerned with the partners balancing upon each other, with some children it might be a sufficient challenge at first just to bear each other's weight. Once the feel of the weight-bearing situation has been experienced with all the demands it makes upon the supporter, the couple should be encouraged to lessen the points of contact until "B" is balancing upon "A" (*See* Plate 23).

While it is not essential that the partners in this task are of the same weight and size, the teacher should be aware that the greater the contrast the more difficult becomes the task if each child is to provide the base in turn, and it might be necessary, therefore, to select certain pairings.

(*d*) *Gaining, holding and losing balance on a partner.*—The next step is taken when "A" adjusts his position so that "B" is guided into the balance and, by a further adjustment, causes "B" to lose balance. The stress in this task is not just on balancing but on ways of gaining and losing balance with both "A" and "B" actively concerned.

At first the child acting as the base will probably offer flat or slightly rounder surfaces on which his partner balances, but if hands are used to grip various body parts, the possibilities are greatly increased.

(*e*) *Lifting, carrying and lowering.*—Tasks concerned with this type of partner work are difficult, particularly when a high standard of performance is demanded. Handling tasks of this nature are obviously suitable for boys, who can usually adapt quite readily to such situations, but the teacher of older Secondary girls might be well advised to consider some of these problems as best being solved in group work where the weight of one is taken by at least two other people. However, with well experienced classes, challenges of lifting, carrying and lowering should be met successfully by both boys and girls.

In order to avoid undue strain and injury, particularly to the back, the child lifting must be able to use his body efficiently and safely. This entails keeping his partner close, getting under him, pushing upwards and using the strength of which the lower half of the body is capable. Furthermore, he needs to hold his partner in such a way that his weight is evenly distributed, that is, balanced about the point of gripping or holding. The partner being lifted also has a vital part to play in such activities; if sufficient introductory work has been given he should be able to hold himself easily and resiliently and in addition be alert and ready to adapt to the changing situation.

The actual carrying of the partner will mean first that the supporter must be in a position from which locomotion can take place, and secondly, that in moving he must not be in danger of losing his hold on his partner. During the carrying the supporter may actually change his grip or alter the situation of his partner, particularly if in lowering he is putting him on to a body part different from when the lifting started.

The lowering process is similar to the lifting one and again great care is needed to ensure that it is done safely and efficiently. Once the partner being lowered has regained contact with the ground, the supporter must maintain his hold and continue to bear part of the weight, relinquishing it only when he feels that his partner is in a position to assume complete control. The one being lowered must prepare the part or parts that are going to receive his weight, otherwise injury might result, particularly if the supporter gives up the weight-bearing too quickly. If the weight is to be taken on to the hands, these need to reach out towards the ground and yield on contact; the amount of "give" will depend upon whether the weight will stay on the hands or be successively transferred to other parts of the body. Plate 24 shows a stage in a lifting, carrying and lowering sequence.

(*f*) *Working in twos to achieve flight.*—Flight is one of the most exhilarating aspects of gymnastics and in partner work it can be achieved by one helping the other. The flight that is gained in this situation should be more than the individual could attain alone, and with the partner's help the actual feeling of flying, of being in the air, is prolonged.

The three stages of flight, the take-off, moving through the air, and the landing will be dealt with separately for clarity, but the helper, besides being able to assist at any one of these three stages, can also aid at two or even at all three phases.

*Take-off.*—The aim of the helper "A" is to assist "B's" take-off, that is, he adds his own force to "B's" powers of ejection. If a preparatory run is needed before the take-off, "A" and "B" can already be in contact and as the point of take-off is reached "A" checks, steadies himself and helps "B" into the air. This travelling together occurs when "A" grips "B's" upper limbs and assists the take-off by an upward push at the point of contact. Another possibility would be for "A" to adopt a suitable position in the take-off area so that "B" travels towards "A," makes contact and the ejection is accomplished.

The ways in which "A" can assist the actual take-off vary considerably, an important factor being which part of his body, feet, back or arms, is being used and which area of "B's" body is going to be contacted. The actions of lifting, pushing, pulling and flinging can be used by "A" and although these actions demand a certain degree of strength, the way in which this added energy is given will differ. Lifting implies that "A" retains his contact with "B" and that during the actual lifting the pressure upwards is maintained, while flinging suggests a sudden explosive movement where contact is quickly lost and "B" is thrown or hurled into the air.

In addition to selecting an appropriate action, in order to assist "B's" upward propulsion, "A" must be able to time his help and to apply it in the right direction. If "A" and "B" are travelling together and "B's" take-off is by an energetic thrust from the lower half of the body which sends him upwards and forwards, "A" must time his action of giving impetus to follow on from this. Thus the original ejection from "B" is immediately superseded by that of "A" and the action continued along the upward and forward direction.

Unless "A" is able to judge correctly the force, the timing and the direction of his action in relation to "B's" own take-off, the result will be impaired flight with "B" being thrown off balance, jerked into the air or even attaining less flight than he would achieve alone.

*Flight.*—The helper "A's" role is again varied. He may keep his hold on "B" during the whole period of flight, resulting in partner-assisted flight. This would involve "A" actually travelling during "B's" flight, pivoting on the spot, or remaining stationary while "B" flies over. It is relevant here to note the difference between carrying a partner and assisting him during flight. In the former the couple remain close together with many parts touching, while in the latter the two are apart with minimal points of contact, so that the partner has an experience of travelling through the air and not one of being lifted.

The helper also has the possibility of "boosting" "B's" flight *en route*. The example of a couple doing a leap-frog action will serve as a useful illustration. If the "back" is sufficiently low for the child going over to place his hands before his feet leave the ground, only a brief period of flight will be gained from pushing against the "back" as he goes over. However, if the latter is comparatively high, the performer will achieve upward flight first from his own take-off and then "boost" this on the way, by pushing against the "back" as he goes over. If the "back" now reacts to "B's" touch not only by resisting the downward push, but also by energetically pushing upward, he adds considerable impetus to "B's" flight.

*Landing.*—When an individual achieves flight, his natural pre-occupation with making a safe landing often inhibits the actual movement through the air. A child assisting his partner in this way can not only help him to land and recover easily and safely, but also, by relieving him of some of the concern of landing, enable him to appreciate the time spent in the air.

If the helper "A" has held his partner during flight the process of aiding the landing follows logically. "A" will be able to control "B's" momentum, help him to regain a vertical position and also, if necessary, to rebound into one or more resilient jumps.

If "B" has had true flight, "A" must take up a well balanced position and reach towards "B," yielding on meeting to lessen the impact. It must be stressed that "A" is not catching "B" (this is a situation which can be exploited safely and to the full in group work) but is concerned with slowing down his partner's momentum and thereby helping him to control his landing.

If this type of partner work is to be of value the child who is in some way being assisted in flight must himself be able to take-off effectively, land safely and control his body in the air. In fact all the considerations of flight when working individually apply to the partner situation. In addition the performer must be able to gain impetus from his helper by means of a strong, vigorous pushing action, and hold the body with light tension away from the support during assisted flight.

Although the helper "A" must be adaptable, his task is made easier and his help is the more effective if "B" is clear in what he intends to do in all stages of flight. It is important that in repeating the flight sequence the actions retain the same rhythm and timing. The performers should be helped through doing, experimenting, observing and discussing to appreciate *how* "A" helps "B's" jump and *when* he does this.

(*g*) *Counter-balance and counter-tension.*—These involve complete interdependence and so a considerable time is needed by the couple in order to explore thoroughly the possibilities within the situation. Their first task would be to find positions in which they could gain a counter-balance or counter-tension and in achieving these positions discover how much to yield to and how much to resist each other's weight. In fact at the beginning, the pair will not so much attain positions but rather come to jerky, see-saw actions where first one and then the other exerts too strong or too weak a pressure.

However, once this stage has been mastered and the pair know how to adjust to each other, they should be encouraged to experiment with different holds and to find out how to cope with asymmetrical situations. Most couples will begin with a hand or wrist grip because this gives a sense of security, with weight on both feet, either pushing towards each other (counter-balance) or pulling away (counter-tension). There are other possibilities, for example, a hand can grip the partner's ankle, or the elbows can be used to get a linking grip. When the hold is other than with two hands it becomes possible for the couple to investigate taking weight on other parts of the body, even becoming inverted. They may find it easier to match their positions at first but eventually an interplay between symmetrical and asymmetrical holds, bases and positions should be experienced.

Plates 25 and 26 show moments of counter-balance and counter-tension. In the latter it is worth noting the use of the head. The whole of the body is actively engaged in pulling away from the partner, but the head, like the free limbs, adds to this pulling action by reaching out in yet another direction.

Within the actual counter-balance and counter-tension, movement can take place. The previous uncontrolled see-saw action can become a deliberate "to-ing and fro-ing" where first one and then the other partner exerts a greater pushing or pulling action. Travelling together is possible, although this depends upon the ease with which the base can be moved, and changes of level can be brought about.

Although the couple will find the actual moments of counter-balance and counter-tension challenging and interesting, there are further progressions for skilled performers. The ways in which the two gain their positions can be considered and also what happens when these positions are lost. It is difficult to give general examples here because the possibilities are many. The main aim of the teacher will be to help the children to feel what is a natural way of gaining a particular counter-balance or counter-tension, and then to appreciate the logical movements which follow once the position has been lost.

## *Apparatus*

Concern for another person in gymnastics is such a new idea for most children that they need considerable time working on the floor during which they can explore thoroughly all the possibilities. To introduce apparatus too soon would complicate matters: the children would not be able to concentrate fully on a partner, the task in hand and the apparatus. It is in such circumstances that accidents could occur. Furthermore, in some instances the partner is used in the beginning stages as an obstacle to be got over or under, and apparatus added to this situation would be superfluous. In the more advanced stages where partners take each other's weight, it is essential that they are given ample time in which to become skilled and thoroughly conversant with the situation. Therefore, no apparatus, other than mats, should be used until the couples are competent and safe in their handling of each other. It is during the floorwork that the teacher helps the children to develop a sense of partnership with real concern for each other, and once this has been attained work on apparatus can begin.

It has been suggested earlier that partner work should not be given in one year but interspersed with other advanced themes. Therefore, the teacher will appreciate that as each new partner situation is introduced, the work on apparatus must always be preceded by floorwork. The teacher will naturally begin with small apparatus and each couple should have one piece only, *e.g.* a skipping rope, and the task should be a simple one. If all the pairs have the same piece of apparatus the teacher will be able to help the whole class generally as well as individuals to answer the task set in a safe and appropriate way.

Once small apparatus and straightforward tasks have been dealt with the progressions are varied but generally it will be a gradual setting of more demanding tasks with more complicated arrangements of apparatus. When planning the apparatus, it should be remembered that it is used to extend a particular partner situation and it should never become so complex that the latter is lost sight of. In the final stages it should be possible for skilled couples to arrange their own apparatus and to set themselves relevant problems.

**Apparatus**—a skipping rope.

*Task* 1.—To share the rope and skip.

If one child holds both ends and does the turning, the other is free to come and go, to rotate and to take up a position face to face, back to back or to the side of his partner. It is also possible for each to hold an end and to skip together or alternately.

Skipping is, of course, a normal playground activity of children, particularly girls, and they often set themselves very difficult tasks with intricate step patterns and rhythms. The value of bringing such activities into the scope of a gymnastic lesson is that although some children already have considerable skill in this respect, it is not true of the majority. Furthermore, in this particular activity two of the desirable aspects of partner work, co-operation and achieving a common timing, are present. In the early stages of acquiring bodily skills the more the gymnastic situation relates to or starts from children's play activities the greater will be the gain in both.

*Task* 2.—One child holds one end of the rope, the other end is free.

The rope can be swung round in a circle, the level of which can vary, while the other child uses it as a moving obstacle either going under or over. This child has to appreciate the possibilities of remaining on the spot, moving round in the opposite direction to the rope, and moving with the rope, and the different timing this entails.

*Task* 3.—One child holds the rope, the other end is tied. N.B. The railings in the playground, chairs and tables in the Hall, and wall bars in the gymnasium can be used.

If the rope is anchored low to the ground and the other end held high or vice versa, the performer has two spaces in which to work, the angle to the ground giving a range of heights. Short repetitive sequences could be invented, going over and under the rope with the possibilities of travelling up and down. In addition, the holder of the rope himself could become an obstacle so that instead of the performer having a forward and backward path, he could now have a circular track during which he goes over his partner. If the holder grips the rope other than with two hands, *e.g.* holds it under his foot or between his knees, he is able to vary the shape of his body so that his partner has a different obstacle to contend with on each circuit.

Finally the child holding the rope could also have a hoop near him or in his free hand, in which case the following possibilities could be considered.

**Apparatus**—one or two hoops.

*Task.*—Two share the apparatus.

The hoop can be placed on the floor and the couple work in a follow-the-leader relationship. In this situation the hoop can be used to get over, by step-like or jumping actions, or with the stress on the area inside and outside, as in hopping in and out. The children need to change from leader to follower frequently and should be encouraged to make their sequences short and repetitive.

"A" could hold the hoop for his partner to get over and through, both from above and below without touching. "A" should experiment with the placing of the hoop; it can be held parallel, at right angles or tilted to the floor and the height can vary considerably. If "B" is given the task of getting through the hoop he has to assess the situation presented by "A" and solve it in his resulting movement. "A" should retain a particular position of the hoop until "B" has found a successful way to answer the set task and then the two can change roles or "A" can give a further challenge by changing either the height or angle of the hoop or both. This is again a true partner situation: the child holding the hoop is actively involved. He knows the task that has been set and he must realise that it is up to him to place the hoop so that his partner can answer the task in a satisfying way. The solving of the problem should not be made too easy or too difficult.

A progression could be that the obstacle, the hoop, is kept moving by "A" so that "B" is faced with a situation that varies. It is important that "A" selects a repetitive action, *e.g.* the hoop can be swung parallel or at right angles to the floor, it can be placed on end and rotated, or it can be raised and lowered. Once "A" has established a rhythm "B" can begin to work. If the task is again to get in and out of the hoop he may need help in judging what is the best point at which to achieve a particular action, *e.g.* jumping in when the hoop is at its lowest, or getting out underneath when it is at its highest.

Further progressions will probably become evident to the teacher whilst taking the preliminary stages. For example, the partner could hold two hoops of the same or different size. They could be placed in similar or different ways either close together or apart, with the possibility of being still or moving.

The teacher must decide at what stage it would be profitable for the children to select actions and perfect sequences. In the latter instance the alternate holding and working, as well as the actual taking and giving up of the hoop, could become an integral part of the final sequence.

**Apparatus**—mats.

*Task.*—Work together sharing a mat.

Mats are useful pieces of apparatus in that they give a definite area for work on floor level. The teacher will often find that couples working together do not use floor space wisely, their pathways tending to meander. Mats, therefore, not only provide a definite area for work but, since the floor immediately surrounding the mat can also be used, they can become the focal point of a sequence.

The task of working in a limited area with another person is difficult for some children, and the teacher may decide that when beginning this type of work only a simple challenge is needed. For example, the task could be for the couple to share the mat whilst crossing and recrossing it. This would not involve any matching or copying but the children would need to avoid each other, by changing direction, stopping, going over or under, and precise actions, such as compact rolling, as well as adaptability would result.

Once experience has been gained in sharing a working area, the four main aspects of partner work given at the beginning of this chapter can be considered, and appropriate tasks selected. The following are four relevant examples:

### 1. COPYING

The task could be to copy a partner's sequence which has been given as an action task to include jumping over the mat, rolling across and going round it with weight taken partly on the hands.

### 2. OBSTACLES

The mat is used as the focal point of the partner work. The partner making the obstacle could take up his position on the mat, the other working towards him from different angles. This situation is useful when one of the two is rolling under bridge shapes. However, if the couple is stressing flight over the obstacle the landings may be made partly off the mat. In this case, particularly in dive rolling over the obstacle, it would be better for the obstacle to position himself at the side of the mat so that landings would be made wholly on it. Once mats are placed, a certain pathway and angle of approach are suggested, so the teacher must decide which position is appropriate to the needs of each particular couple.

3. MATCHING

Here the couple may be limited entirely to the mat if it is a large one, or to the mat and the space around it. The starting positions, side by side on the mat or opposite each other at the edge of the mat, could be dictated.

4. WEIGHT BEARING

The problem could be one of helping the partner to achieve flight over the mat (both widthwise and lengthwise). The couple would decide whether help should be given at take-off or during flight and positions at the side of or on the mat taken up accordingly. However, as with flight over an obstacle, if the teacher decided that the flight attained by the couple warranted the use of the mat as a landing aid he would re-word the task, getting flight from a distance on to the mat.

**Apparatus**—a form.

*Task.*—To work sharing the apparatus.

Forms also provide a focal point for partner work, but they can be used in other ways. When placed on the floor a form gives a change of level, with a wide or narrow surface and a large space above and a small space underneath. In partner work all these opportunities can be exploited. The following are typical tasks each concerned with one of the four basic partner situations.

1. COPYING

A movement task can be given, such as travelling along and across the form showing symmetrical and asymmetrical actions and the resulting sequence may be copied partly or wholly by the partner.

2. OBSTACLES

The form may be considered as an additional obstacle (*e.g.* when selecting pathways which go over the form and under the partner) or as giving added height to the normal partner–obstacle situation. In the latter circumstance it would be possible for three couples to use the form at once with the obstacles on the form and the partners approaching from either side. If a form is available for each couple, a task of starting at opposite ends, working towards each other and passing midway, would probably result in the pair going under and over each other. However, this challenge could also be solved by a swivelling counter-tension in order to change places.

## 3. MATCHING

If the task is one of matching both actions and pathways the following starting positions could be dictated or suggested by the teacher. An inventive class would readily find their own variations.

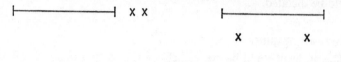

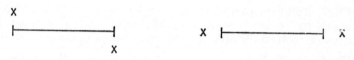

## 4. WEIGHT BEARING

When the form is used narrow side uppermost, partners can work on various aspects of balancing each other, including counter-tension positions. On the broad side of the form all the situations concerned with one helping the other to balance can be repeated, the slightly higher level making this a challenging progression for most children. Flight over or off the form, with the helper standing either at the side of, or on, the form is also a logical progression from the floor work.

Combinations of mats and forms can be used to give variety to the partner situation. Similarly, if forms are hooked at one end on to wall bars, tubular bars, window ladders and bar boxes, or planks hooked on to frames and stools, then additional possibilities of using the variation in height, the slope and the larger space underneath are given.

Although the four main aspects of partner work can still be considered when planning arrangements of *large apparatus*, it is of significance to note that these are not now of equal importance.

## 1. COPYING

If the couples are still at the stage of copying a part or the whole of each other's sequences and as yet have had no experience of further partner situations, with a few possible exceptions they are not ready for work on large apparatus. The copying situation is usually one of transition from working as an individual to being one of a pair and this can be most profitably explored in floor work or with small apparatus. Furthermore, to put children in the position of having to copy a partner's action on large apparatus could be dangerous and, for many, an impossible task.

However, there are two instances in which it might be worth while to give partners the task of copying the essence or the whole of each other's sequence on large apparatus.

With a class inexperienced in the partner situation but able to cope with themselves on apparatus, the teacher could challenge the couples to copy tracks or selected actions. This would be a means of gaining new ideas and serve as a useful introduction to the more demanding partner work.

In addition it is often of value to give skilled, experienced gymnasts such tasks. If the apparatus is arranged as a circuit giving ample opportunities for various tracks, an individual copying another's sequence would probably experience new pathways, actions and rhythms.

When confronted with an arrangement of large pieces of apparatus the partners often start by finding out what each can do. They copy ideas, actions and pathways as a preliminary to answering the task set. However, this is a stage which is passed through quickly and once the pair have explored the possibilities of the apparatus they begin to work in conjunction, with all the "give and take" this entails.

## 2. OBSTACLES

This too is an aspect of partner work best pursued on the floor or with small apparatus. The large apparatus itself normally offers a sufficient challenge, so that there is little point in partner obstacles being the main stress. Even so, when working on the more difficult tasks and problems given below the couple will incidentally use their previous experience of going under or over each other. This occurs when their pathways cross or they need to overtake.

## 3. MATCHING

In selecting apparatus for this type of work the teacher must decide if he is going to:

(a) dictate starting positions and/or pathways,
(b) suggest them by the lay out, or
(c) give couples the opportunity to set their own apparatus or pathways or both.

In (a) and (b) all the various possibilities of starting positions and resulting pathways must be considered and catered for. It will be appreciated that certain pieces of apparatus provide ideal opportunities for a couple to work side by side, with parallel pathways (*See*

Plate 27). Ropes, bars, single or double, with or without saddles, window ladders, wall bars and Cave Southampton "side walls" can be used in this respect, with the couple starting and working side by side, forwards, backwards, or up and down. Apart from using single pieces in this way, apparatus can be placed to form a continuous straight or angled pathway, thus allowing the two to work from opposite ends or to start one in front of the other with the possibility of overtaking. The following is a selection of apparatus arrangements with tasks related to the main idea of partners matching their movements.

**Apparatus**—two forms, box and mats.

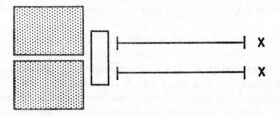

*Task.*—Start at the points indicated and *either* work parallel to each other *or* the pathways can cross on the box.

**Apparatus**—two forms and a horse.

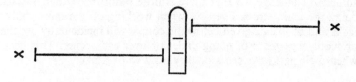

*Task.*—Start at "x," meet on the horse and pass each other to finish in partner's starting position.

**Apparatus**—buck astride a form.

*Task.*—Start at opposite ends of the form, cross by going over and under the buck.

**Apparatus**—inclined form to bar box and mat.

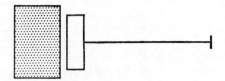

*Task*.—Both start at the same place, work one behind the other matching simultaneously or in canon, using various pathways.

**Apparatus**—one buck, two forms and two mats.

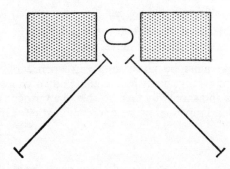

*Task*.—Own choice of starting position and pathway but at some point both must share the same piece of apparatus.

**Apparatus**—double bars and two forms.

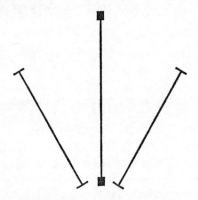

*Task*.—To use all the pieces of apparatus in a matching sequence. The bars give the opportunities of matching actions at different levels, or working side by side or matching in canon.

**Apparatus**—ropes, horse (without pommels) and mat.

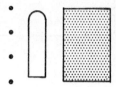

*Task.*—To work side by side from ropes to horse and on to mat. (The difficulty here is to time the swing and the arrival.)

**Apparatus**—double bars and ropes.

    *Task.*—By means of one or two ropes arrive on the bars, use and leave them with matching movements.

The children must be given ample experience of working on teacher-selected arrangements before going on to choose apparatus for themselves and should by then be able to appreciate the different possibilities that individual pieces and combinations can offer.

### 4. WEIGHT BEARING

Up to this stage the teacher would have given the children specific experience in all aspects of the partner situation by means of carefully selected progressions. Both on the floor and on small apparatus the children will have gained in skill and understanding by working at tasks where one aspect of taking each other's weight has been stressed. It is still possible to work in this way on large apparatus.

**Apparatus**—two pieces placed apart.

    *Task.*—To help the partner across the gap by assisting his flight in some way.

**Apparatus**—two pieces one placed beneath the other, *e.g.* high and low bars, or trapeze and mat or ropes and form. The distance between the two pieces should not be great.

    *Task.*—To aid the partner by lifting him from the low piece to the high piece and to help him down by lowering.

**Apparatus**—a narrow surface, flat or inclined, *e.g.* bars, window ladder away from the wall, bar box or form hooked on to bars.

    *Task.*—To travel along or up the narrow surface together maintaining a counter-tension.

Plate 26

PLATE 26.—An example of partner work with counter-tension

PLATE 27.—Ten-year-olds matching actions on apparatus

Plate 27

Plate 28

Plate 29

However, it will be found that as the apparatus gets larger and more complex so the couples will quite naturally select from their past experience appropriate ways of managing each other's weight and not pursue just one aspect. An example of this would be if "A" helped his partner "B" at take-off to arrive on a box. In this position, by means of counter-tension "B" could lift "A" to his level; retaining the counter-tension "A" could now lower "B" to the floor and the latter could assist "A's" landing from a jump off the box. In this particular example assisted take-off, lifting and lowering by use of counter-tension and assisted landing would have taken place. Plates 28 and 29 show moments of counter-tension and lifting and lowering within a sequence.

In the following arrangements of apparatus a problem is presented to the couple, both verbally and in the actual set up of the apparatus, which they solve in their own way.

**Apparatus**—bar at medium level.

*Task.*—Find and perfect ways of helping each other over or on to and off.

**Apparatus**—three pieces of apparatus of differing size and height arranged in a triangle with gaps between.

*Task.*—To use various ways of assisting each other to cross the gaps.

**Apparatus**—a high piece of apparatus.

*Task.*—To find ways of helping each other on to and off the apparatus from above and below.

Work on large apparatus where the partners are continually adjusting to each other's weight is one of the most skilled aspects of gymnastics. Eventually the children should be able to select their own apparatus and set their own problems, but before this stage is reached a high degree of skill in individual body management must have been acquired and all the progressive partner situations experienced.

The organisation of apparatus for partner work needs careful planning. In the first stage each couple will have the same piece of apparatus, *e.g.* a hoop. Later it may be necessary to divide the class, *e.g.* half the couples working on mats the other half on forms. With large apparatus in an average gymnasium, it is possible either for each couple to have their own piece, remembering that wall bars and inclined forms can augment the large portable and fixed apparatus, or if long tracks of apparatus have been arranged, for two or three couples to share the same piece.

L

The teacher should also bear in mind when devising apparatus for other gymnastic themes that it is useful to retain one section at which, as each group arrives, they divide into couples and continue partner work.

In giving children experience of partner work it is as well for the teacher to anticipate certain developments.

Firstly, as soon as a child who hitherto has only worked as an individual is put into the partner situation, one can expect that child's own movement to deteriorate. This is natural because the attention is not on his own body but directed towards his partner. The phase lasts until the child begins to feel at home in the partnership and then the previous bodily skill is shown and in many cases increased.

Secondly, many teachers used to the comparative quiet of individuals working become alarmed at the noise that partner work brings. Obviously a "working" noise is desirable and partners will want to discuss their problems. However, the teacher must help the children to realise that too much discussion and planning, particularly at the beginning, results in a re-hash of old ideas, whereas by doing and experimenting new ways will be discovered. The answers to all movement tasks lie to a great degree in doing rather than discussing. The teacher will also need to be alert to the various partner situations before him, because often with his intervention and help the couple can be encouraged to pursue a worthwhile idea rather than abandon it. Generally, the partners will find out for themselves by a process of trial and error which movement possibilities are relevant to the situation.

Thirdly, it must be appreciated that all this takes time. If the children are pressed too soon for finished sequences, the teacher will find the resulting work poor and lacking in invention. Work in twos takes at least twice as long as individual work to arrive at any degree of completion and in any case it is the actual working out of the situation that is of value in the preliminary stages.

Fourthly, it is usual for the first results of partner work to be long, involved sequences. It seems that even though as individuals children have appreciated what is appropriate in their own work, when put into the partner situation they once more revert to stringing ideas together with little regard for movement logic. Although they have learnt to select from their own ideas they find this difficult at first with a partner and so nearly everything the pair discover is retained. It is only through doing, observing and discussing that they develop a feel for what is logical and right in the movement sense.

The ability to work well with another person is a significant stage of achievement in gymnastics and both the teacher and children should be aware of this. It is essential that the teacher knows his class before embarking upon the idea and that he is able to give the children a worthwhile experience. The couples should be led through the progressive stages and aspects of partner work so that they acquire new skills and further their understanding. Only if children have been well taught and have developed mutual care and consideration will they be able to work profitably and safely together and thereby gain in enjoyment, skill and understanding.

# CHAPTER 10

# ADVANCED BODY MANAGEMENT

THIS is not a gymnastic theme in the sense that new material is presented. The movement experience is widened by relating and developing aspects of the work previously considered at an elementary or intermediate level. The skills acquired in the early stages are adapted and augmented in the light of new situations.

A teacher who considers his class capable of tackling and profiting from advanced work probably knows, through observation, the themes he wishes to revise and develop. Therefore this material is given in the form of suggestions for furthering bodily skill and understanding, and enriching a basic vocabulary.

## Relating elementary and intermediate body management themes

Since the skilled performer should be able to consider more than one movement concept at a time the themes experienced in isolation at the beginning can now be correlated. There are many ways of doing this.

EXAMPLE 1.

A task is selected that each child can answer at his own level and the resulting action taken as the climax of a phrase, with other movement ideas being considered in turn. In other words, one action is "played" with, using different movement emphases.

If "choose an inverted balance" is given as a task, some children will produce familiar skills such as handstands, headstands and shoulderstands, but there are many possibilities, particularly when the shape of the body is other than elongated and the base is not restricted to like parts. Once the action is clarified the following tasks could be taken separately, the teacher deciding whether all or a few sequences are to be perfected.

Task 1.—By rolling forwards or backwards get into and out of the balance.

Task 2.—Spring into and out of the balance. (The first part of the task is not possible with all inverted balances.)

Task 3.—Try to move the base and retain the balance. (This would result in walking on the hands or pivoting on the head and hands or shoulders.)

*Task* 4.—Experiment with various body shapes—curled, elongated and spread while inverted.

*Task* 5.—Terminate your balance by twisting or turning.

*Task* 6.—Gain and lose your balance with a symmetrical stress throughout; repeat asymmetrically.

*Task* 7.—Invent a sequence in which your particular inverted balance is achieved three times. Gain and lose each balance with a different movement emphasis.

## EXAMPLE 2

Another way of relating basic ideas would be to emphasise a part of the body and to see how this part is used in various gymnastic situations. For example, legs can be important in actions on the floor and apparatus.

They can—

(*a*) take the body from place to place as in running and stepping,

(*b*) lower and raise the body through different levels,

(*c*) eject and receive the whole weight as in flight,

(*d*) initiate actions such as twists, turns, loss of balance,

(*e*) provide the impetus in swivelling and pivoting actions,

(*f*) add momentum to swinging actions on ropes or bars,

(*g*) support the body as in gripping a trapeze or bar.

These will not be new actions to most children but by associating actions which have a common idea, movement understanding is furthered. Tasks could be set demanding an emphasis on legs throughout a sequence with at least two different ways of using them included.

## EXAMPLE 3

It would also be possible to take one aspect such as twisting and see how it is related to other movement ideas, *e.g.* twisting and changes of direction,

and changes of speed,
in locomotion and stillness,
during flight,
between different levels,
with a partner.

It is impracticable to enumerate all the ways in which the basic themes could be considered as a whole but it is imperative that the teacher sets out to widen the children's movement experience. Once a class has a certain degree of skill it is easy to embark upon ideas which result in "body tricks" instead of extending an understanding of objective work.

### Developing elementary body management themes

Although a teacher may decide to return to basic gymnastic work for a more detailed exploration there are three themes capable of considerable development at an advanced level. These are weight-bearing, stillness, and locomotion, certain aspects of which result in balance and flight. Both involve much material and are dealt with separately in the following two chapters.

### Apparatus

In selecting apparatus at this stage the teacher should ensure that it adds considerably to any action or movement challenge.

(a) Dissimilar pieces could be used in one arrangement, giving a variety of height, width and surface.

(b) Spaces between pieces could be wide so that flight or assisted flight can take place.

(c) Springboards and trampettes could be used frequently.

(d) Skilled performers could be given apparatus which they arrange themselves in order to answer a specific task.

(e) Individuals and groups can be allowed to select and arrange their own apparatus and set their own task.

(f) Mobile situations could be given.

In the latter, where for example, a form is hooked on to a trapeze or between two rope ladders, a completely new situation is presented. To work on apparatus that swings freely at one or both ends could be dangerous, but it is an arrangement in which competent gymnasts can revel and gain considerable satisfaction and enjoyment.

**Apparatus**—medium or high box.

*Task.*—Arrive on the box by means of a roll. Leave the box by using a forward or backward roll.

This is a progression from the elementary stage where rolling on apparatus is confined to one level or between the floor and low apparatus. Further progressions could be rolling up and down inclined surfaces, and along narrow apparatus, and if a springboard or trampette is added flight can precede the roll on.

**Apparatus**—horse with one pommel.

*Task* 1.—Get on and off asymmetrically.

*Task* 2.—Arrive on, using the pommel to gain an asymmetrical balance.

*Task* 3.—Using the pommel, experiment with ways of twisting over and back.

Some horses can be raised or lowered at one end so that a slope results. This adds considerably to tasks involving getting on, off and over.

**Apparatus**—mattress over two forms.

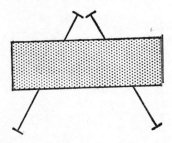

*Task.*—By rolling, traverse the mattress lengthwise with continuity.

This is a deceptive arrangement, for the bumps and the gap between the forms necessitate compact and elongated rolling in order to achieve any degree of continuity.

**Apparatus**—low and high bar, with a form inclined to the low bar, a saddle on the top bar, and a box on the far side.

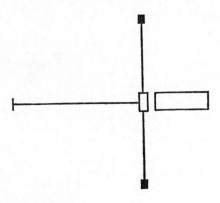

*Task.*—Use the apparatus to produce symmetrical and asymmetrical actions.

**Apparatus**—a form inclined to a high bar, trampette and box, one mat.

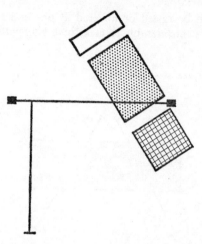

*Task.*—To produce two tracks, one clockwise, the other anti-clockwise, showing continuity.

**Apparatus**—a form hooked at one end to a low trapeze, rings or rope ladder. N.B. It may be necessary to tie the form if the hooks appear unstable, and to place a mat under the end of the form to prevent the floor being marked.

*Task 1.*—Invent a rhythmical sequence going on to and off the swinging form.

*Task 2.*—Show ways of getting under and over the moving form.

*Task 3.*—Experiment with balancing positions while the form is in motion.

CHAPTER 11

# GAINING, MAINTAINING AND LOSING BALANCE

BALANCING, the ability to hold the body over a comparatively small base, is a fundamental gymnastic skill.

At pre-school age the child is concerned with standing, that is, maintaining an upright position, and then walking and running. The Primary school child is still actively occupied with exploring balancing possibilities. He pares down his base, walking on toes or heels, deliberately chooses to walk along narrow surfaces, and tries out ways of balancing on parts other than feet.

The natural desire to balance the body and to achieve a high degree of control within these actions is exploited in gymnastics.

## *Material*

Although balance is not stressed as such in acquiring elementary body skill, weight bearing and stillness, the two movement ideas which together bring about equilibrium, are explored thoroughly. Balance is considered here as an advanced theme but the beginnings of balance are found in the basic ways of managing the body. It is impossible to say at what point weight bearing ends and balancing begins, since this depends upon the skill of the performer and the part acting as the base. However, it is important that the base is diminished, giving a feeling of perching, not resting, on a part, and that the stress is upward, away from the base. If a stable balance is held skilfully and not "moved through" stillness results.

In order to clarify balancing actions it is useful to consider the three phases of gaining, maintaining and losing balance.

### GAINING BALANCE

Stability results from the centre of gravity being vertically over the base or the basal area. The body is most stable when the hips, the region of the centre of gravity in the normal upright position, take the weight, but usually this would be weight bearing and not balancing. Therefore, the support is composed of other body parts, and in order to achieve equilibrium the hips must be placed above the base.

Certain factors facilitate balance; large, flat areas of the body such as the shoulders provide stable bases. Similarly, when two parts form

155

a base it is easier if these are the same and placed symmetrically. Three or more parts can constitute a base but the greater the number used and the further apart they are, the more the action tends towards weight bearing. Conversely, pin point, narrow and asymmetrical bases make balancing more difficult.

The ways in which balanced positions are gained vary. In order to achieve an upright balance it is usual for a weight-bearing situation to be assumed and then the base diminished. Inverted balances require an initial action to get the body over the selected base and this is often accomplished by kicking up or swinging the legs. Skilled gymnasts can lever into a balance or arrive in a balance from flight. The degree of speed and energy required to gain a balance depend upon the action and the performer, but there is normally a deceleration and a controlling of energy as the point of balance is reached.

MAINTAINING BALANCE

Once a state of balance has been gained the focus is on keeping it. There is a "point of balance" when the centre of gravity is vertically over the centre of the base. There is also an "area of balance." This is found by shifting the centre of gravity above the base, exploring the possible range of movement while balance is maintained.

The shape of the body can vary while a balance is held; curled, elongated, spread and twisted positions all being possible. During a balance, small adjusting movements will be taking place all the time, therefore it is important to note that a spread position allows greater freedom of movement than does a compact one.

The appropriate tension required to hold the body in balance, particularly during inversion, must be maintained throughout the action. It is inability to sustain this tension for any length of time that can cause a loss of balance.

LOSING BALANCE

Balance is lost when the centre of gravity is moved outside the base. For beginners this is synonymous with unintentional loss of control or going through a balance. Skilled performers can terminate a balance in two ways. Firstly, the balance can be ended by a controlled moving into another position. The centre of gravity is kept over the base until a free body part is placed ready to share the weight bearing. The downward levering action of the legs out of a handstand is an example of this.

Secondly, the balance can be followed by a loss of control which would result in a fall if the gymnast were unable to recapture command of his body. Deliberate loss of balance followed by regaining control can be brought about in three ways. The centre of gravity can be shifted outside the base by tipping the body in any direction, momentum being gained as balance is lost. The free limbs can execute a strong, quick whipping action which immediately brings about unbalance. The base itself can be moved by a vigorous pushing action. The examples describe how a balance on hands could be followed by a momentary loss of control.

(a) The legs begin the tilting action which pulls the hips out of line and balance is lost.

(b) The legs part and whip round in a twisting action causing the centre of gravity to shift outside the base.

(c) The arms flex and the hands push against the floor, throwing the body out of balance.

As stillness is associated with balance so transference of weight and locomotion result from loss of balance.

## Teaching

In a gymnastic lesson balancing actions of necessity include all three phases mentioned above. Recognition of the difficulties which will probably be encountered by beginners and unskilled performers is of value to the teacher.

When more than one part constitutes the base these parts are sometimes placed too close or too far apart in relation to the rest of the body. Often there is little awareness of the relation of other parts to the base, the hips particularly being out of line. When the balance is on hands the shoulders need to be stabilised and the counterbalancing action of the free limbs appreciated. The beginner is rarely able to feel the "point of balance" and "the area of balance" and the play between the two. Similarly, when trying to hold a balance there is a tendency to make wild correcting movements which cause overbalance.

The tensions involved in balance are new to the beginner. He needs to feel the muscular control required to hold each position and in doing so will err between too much and too little. Sometimes there is an inability to push away from the base and collapsing results. Inverted balances require an initial forceful action to achieve the upside down position. Beginners find difficulty in selecting a suitable speed to get into a balance and can rarely decelerate as the point of balance is approached.

There will invariably be some children whose failure to hold all but the simple balances is not due to any of these reasons. Fear of being and staying in an unusual position, particularly upside down, and most common of all, fear of toppling over and falling can be most inhibiting. Such children need careful, patient help and their confidence must be built up over many lessons with the teacher guiding each stage rather than forcing the pace.

This raises the question of whether an individual should be helped to experience the "feel" of balancing so that he can eventually perform such skills unaided. The teacher, a partner and apparatus can provide different kinds of "support" and this must be considered as a legitimate means of helping a child to achieve balancing actions.

The teacher should be able to give most help verbally. He may need to stand by an apprehensive child in order to give moral support, but the need to give physical support should be rare. Partner work, where one helps the other to balance, can be invaluable if the situation is sympathetically controlled by the teacher. (*See* the chapter on Partner Work.) The way in which apparatus can be arranged so that balancing is experienced safely is discussed later in this chapter.

Most children will naturally acquire balancing skills if they are led through the progressive stages and never put into a position of danger. The experience of gaining, holding and losing a simple shoulder balance can be built upon as more advanced balances are attempted. Growing bodily skill and the resulting increase in confidence appear to be the relevant factors contributing towards the mastery of difficult balances, including those of inversion.

It is vital that the teacher appreciates what constitutes skill in balance. The skilled performer is able to take up, maintain and lose a balance at will. He can select from a variety of bases and show versatility in the way he arrives in a balance, for example, from flight or by levering. The gymnast who is confident in his balancing ability does not show the strain of the beginner and his movements to adjust the balance are small and precise.

Once confidence in balancing is achieved, playing with the action can be enjoyed. The feeling of instability is not frightening but exhilarating, and the body can be deliberately thrown off balance because control can be regained when necessary. This is also a great safety factor. Many accidents result from loss of balance and falling, and a child who has experienced instability can react to correct the situation. (*See* Chapter 12 for off-balance flight.)

The poise and the ease with which the expert balances are obvious and his economy of movement and effort the result of accumulated skill. The poise of the body is not only a gymnastic concern. Those children who, through moving, have recognised what balance entails should be able to draw upon this experience in other situations.

FLOOR TASKS

> *Task* 1.—Take weight on an area of the trunk. Try to get as much of your body as you can off the floor until you are perched on just a part of your original base.
>
> *Task* 2.—Take weight on both feet, diminish your base until you are balancing on part of the foot or feet.

*Task* 3.—Find out which parts of your legs you can use as a base for balancing.

*Task* 4.—Try to achieve at least a momentary balance on hands.

Progressions could be concerned with:

experimenting with bases composed of two or more parts,
finding out the implications of using wide, narrow and pin-point bases,
playing with changing body shapes above the base,
inventing sequences where at least two different balance positions are included.

As children become adept at balancing, less movement occurs and the teacher must avoid a slowing down of the lesson pace. It could be relevant here to refer to and recall the previous experience of locomotion and stillness, the latter having now developed into balance. The actions preceding and following a balance must be considered as soon as the basic idea has been understood, therefore tasks should be given requiring balances in a phrase or sequence of movement.

*Task* 1.—Select one balance; find various ways of moving into it, and out of it.

*Task* 2.—Try to gain inverted balances with bases consisting of unlike parts, such as hand and forearm. Select two or more, and invent a sequence where the loss of one balance leads into another.

Progressions would lead naturally to the perfecting of sequences involving various balances with the stress on how each balance is gained and lost.

## *Apparatus*

The use of apparatus in balance considerably widens the scope of the work. Apparatus that is inclined, narrow, slippery, high, moving and at different levels provides balancing problems not encountered at floor level. All parts of the body cannot act as a base on the floor but bar-like apparatus enables hips to be used, and in this situation body parts can be below the base, which is impossible in floor work. At ground level the base has to be flat or nearly so but when using the pommels, ropes, bars, trapeze, rings, wall bars and the narrow side of forms, the supporting parts can grip.

The value of apparatus as a means of helping children to feel a balance position such as inversion has been mentioned. This point is worth the teacher's consideration. Many children will not balance upside down on the floor but will try with a support or something to grip. This enables them to experience the orientation involved in inversion and yet feel safe while doing so.

Balance is included in partner work where one helps the other to balance, and counter-balancing situations occur. (*See* Chapter 9 on Partner Work.) When arranging apparatus the teacher may decide to have one group working in twos on these ideas.

It must be stressed that balancing on apparatus demands a skilled used of the body. A few of the tasks suggested could be tackled profitably by beginners as part of their basic gymnastic experience. The majority of the tasks are for children who already possess a certain degree of competence and skill.

### JUNIORS

Younger Juniors are interested in balancing while moving on apparatus and this should be catered for. Older Juniors can tackle pure balancing tasks; some may be able to arrive on apparatus in a balance, and most will be able to balance once on apparatus and get off by losing balance.

**Apparatus**—individual mats, mats and mattresses.

*Task 1.*—Cross the mat holding one balance.

*Task 2.*—Balance at the side of the mat, cross it and finish in a balance at the other side.

**Apparatus**—stilts.

*Task.*—In the playground a group can use stilts at various heights to practise balance walking.

**Apparatus**—two forms, narrow side uppermost and placed parallel, close together.

*Task.*—Tasks concerning balance walking as well as using hands and feet can be given. Height has been added to the balance situation but since the forms are used together the problem of placing the supports in a straight line is omitted.

**Apparatus**—form, narrow side uppermost.

*Tasks.*—This apparatus gives opportunities for balance walking with height; the added difficulty is to place the supports along a straight line on a narrow surface. The introductory tasks involving travelling on hands and feet, as well as feet only, could be supplemented with travelling in different directions and changing direction, once a certain degree of proficiency is achieved. Working backwards along such apparatus takes time and queues might arise so it may be expedient to combine a form and a mat task.

**Apparatus**—two or more horizontally suspended ropes across the gymnasium or hall.

*Tasks.*—Horizontal ropes can be used for balance walking and scrambling, the movement of the ropes being an extra consideration.

**Apparatus**—high, horizontal ladders, poles and planks.

*Tasks.*—This type of apparatus is ideal for moving and balancing activities. The narrow surface and the height require courage and give a sense of daring.

**Apparatus**—inclined slippery planks or forms.

*Tasks.*—Such apparatus allows for combined sliding and balancing activities. The body is balanced over the selected base while the sliding movement takes place.

**Apparatus**—low stools, box tops, steps, stage blocks.

*Task 1.*—Balance on the apparatus; use a free part to lead you on to the floor.

*Task 2.*—Get on to and off the apparatus, at one point hold a balance.

*Task 3.*—Balance upside down at the side of the apparatus, lower your legs and place them on the apparatus, get on and jump off.

**Apparatus**—boxes, stools, or stage blocks at hip height.

*Task 1.*—Start and finish away from the apparatus. Get on and off achieving one balance on the apparatus and one on the floor.

*Task 2.*—Lie on the apparatus, place your hands on the floor and with the apparatus as a support try to take weight and balance on your hands.

*Task 3.*—Arrive on the apparatus feet first, hands to touch the floor first in coming off; include at least one balance.

SECONDARY

These problems require considerable skill, some being only for advanced performers. If the teacher has assessed the ability of his class correctly there should be little danger in attempting such tasks.

**Apparatus**—mats.

> *Task* 1.—Experiment with inverted balances—choose one and find how you can achieve and lose it.
>
> *Task* 2.—Roll into and out of a balance.

**Apparatus**—forms.

> *Task* 1.—Grip the sides of the form and experiment with various inverted balances.
>
> *Task* 2.—Try out balances with the base divided between the floor and the form.

**Apparatus**—form narrow side uppermost.

> *Task* 1.—Travel along the form balancing on different parts of the body.
>
> *Task* 2.—Travel across the form, achieving a balance on the form.

**Apparatus**—low inclined forms.

> *Task* 1.—Travel down the form holding at least two balances.
>
> *Task* 2.—Travel on a zigzag pathway up the form, balancing upon the two levels.

**Apparatus**—bars, hip height.

> *Task* 1.—Balance on the hips with or without hands gripping. Experiment with ways of getting into and out of one balance.
>
> *Task* 2.—Balance on the hips, place hands on the floor and with the bar as a support try to hold an inverted balance.
>
> *Task* 3.—Arrive poised on the bar. Travel along the bar using the floor as necessary and include two other held balances.

**Apparatus**—two bars, low and high.

> *Task* 1.—Balance on the top bar, resolve the balance to arrive on the low bar and balance there.
>
> *Task* 2.—Experiment with balances using a divided base between the floor and the low bar, or between the two bars.

**Apparatus**—box top, or mattress over a form, or low bar.

> *Task* 1.—Balance on the apparatus using parts of the lower half of the body as a base, tip to lose balance, land and roll.

When working on losing balance the apparatus must be very low if the original base is provided by the hips or part of the legs. This is because when the body is tipped, it is the hands, arms and shoulders which receive the weight and to do so from height might result in injury. Conversely, when the balance is on the upper half of the body the apparatus should be high. This allows the tipping action to be prolonged and there is sufficient space for the body to regain the upright position and land safely on the feet. As skill increases the apparatus in each case can be raised or lowered.

**Apparatus**—box, horse or buck, full height.

> *Task.*—Balance on hands on the apparatus, tip and land feet first on the mat.

**Apparatus**—two ropes.

> *Tasks.*—Tasks resulting in inverted balances where the hands grip the ropes help to give the orientation experience mentioned earlier.

**Apparatus**—box, horse or buck, hip height.

> *Tasks.*—Such apparatus can also be used to give support to inverted balances. The performer starts on the apparatus and places the hands on the floor near to the apparatus. The weight is then shifted gradually on to the hands with the apparatus providing support at hip level.

**Apparatus**—swinging apparatus such as ropes, trapeze, rings and rope ladders.

> *Tasks.*—This apparatus can be used in conjunction with balancing tasks. The problems of balance are increased considerably when the apparatus is moving.

**Apparatus**—box, three or four layers.

> *Task.*—Jump on to the box and hold your arrival; get off by gaining and losing an inverted balance.

**Apparatus**—ropes to box.

> *Task.*—Swing to arrive in a balanced position on the box, get off with weight on hands.

**Apparatus**—ropes to bar or narrow form.

> *Task.*—Swing to land poised on the narrow piece of apparatus, tip off and roll. The logical progression which follows arriving in a balance from a swing, is to arrive in a balance after flight— *see* Chapter 12.

M

**Apparatus**—high bar, high box and a low box, three mats.

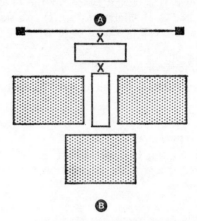

*Task* 1.—Achieve a balance on each piece of apparatus within a sequence.

*Task* 2.—Travel from A to B showing a balance on each level.

*Task* 3.—Choose your own pathway but your sequence must include divided balances at the points marked "X".

**Apparatus**—two forms, a buck and a mat.

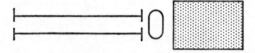

*Task* 1.—Travel along *both* forms including at least two held balances. An inverted balance is to be used to get off the buck.

*Task* 2.—Balance on the forms and tip off to each side in turn. Slide over the buck into an inverted balance on the mat.

**Apparatus**—horse, springboard, and a box top placed on a mattress.

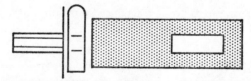

*Task*.—Arrive on the horse balanced with weight on hands, achieve a balance with a divided base on the mattress and box. Aim for continuity between the balances.

CHAPTER 12

# THE BODY IN FLIGHT

FLIGHT occurs when the body moves unsupported through the air. Jumping is a natural action, particularly of the young: children jump for joy and through excitement, accenting the upward, or they jump when thwarted and frustrated, stressing the downward part of the action. There is a basic desire to overcome gravity and being in the air gives a sense of freedom.

Flight can be considered as a form of locomotion when the stress is on travelling through the air, or as a way of transferring weight when the stress is on the part or parts used for take-off and landing. In advanced flight the actions of the body whilst airborne are more important. Being in the air is a unique situation, and in gymnastics flight is exploited and developed to a high degree, giving the work one of its essential characteristics.

## *Material*

In considering flight three phases become apparent—the take-off, the actual flight and the landing.

### TAKE-OFF

The aim is to get the body into the air and to do this gravity has to be overcome. The legs are the main ejectors and although other parts can be used it is the lower half of the body which, by nature of its construction, is most efficient in projecting the body into the air.

The action of the body at take-off can be likened to a series of hinges and springs which are compressed and then released. The take-off considered here is from the feet but the principles are the same whatever part is used. Ankles, knees and hips flex and by thrusting against the floor or apparatus eject the body into the air. The flexing is comparatively slow, in preparation for the main action. The extension is executed quickly and during it the "pent up" tension is released, resulting in a vigorous, explosive effort. The change from flexion into extension is vital in any take-off. Small jumps may require only a partial flexion of ankles, knees and hips; large jumps will necessitate full use of the ejecting mechanism. The preparation will always be downward and the thrust upward, but the latter might be modified to forwards and upwards according to the desired direction of flight.

The upper part of the body joins in the downward flexing action

165

and the chest, particularly the "centre of levity" becomes important in the upward thrust.

## FLIGHT

Flight begins as soon as the body has left the ground. The great outburst of energy required at take-off should be dissolved, otherwise the body is strained and the freedom of being airborne lost. Throughout flight a slight tension should be maintained in the whole body, but particularly in the head and chest so that there is a sense of moving easily through the air. The skilled performer can experience the moment of suspension, when the body appears to hover between the upward surge and the downward drop.

If the take-off has been effective the whole body will be stretched. This extended position is needed on landing and so can be held throughout flight, but there are other possibilities. Twisting and turning can occur, provided that these have been initiated in the take-off. The shape of the body can be altered by tucking, spreading and arching, while the possibilities of symmetrical and asymmetrical positions are virtually unlimited.

The direction and trajectory of the flight can vary. The usual direction is forward but flight backwards, sideways and diagonally is possible. When the body is tipped diagonally, the vertical position is lost and off-balance occurs. The pathway through the air can be one where distance gained or height achieved is emphasised, with variations between.

## LANDING

Although it is possible to land on various parts of the body, the feet, with the rest of the lower half, usually perform this function. In order to achieve safe landings, certain actions are essential. Technically the landing begins as contact between body and floor is made, but there must be a preparation for this moment while the body is still in the air. The preparation consists of an extension towards the landing area so that on contact the body can yield easily, acting as a shock absorber.

The way in which the landing is effected will depend upon what the body has been doing during flight. In landing from a height the body will drop deeply with an action of maximum "give." If the flight has considerable forward momentum, the impetus of the body as it lands will cause an immediate transference of weight continuing in the same direction. Such landings are also necessary as a safety measure when turning and tipping have taken place during flight. When a small area of the body is the first part to make contact, as in a one foot landing, injury could result unless the weight is transferred immediately on to the other foot and continued into a running action, or on to other parts resulting in rolling.

Since the landing action is similar to the flexion prior to take-off, the resilient capacity of the body can be exploited and it can be sent up into another jump. This means that the slight tension achieved during flight is not dispersed on landing but recharged during the brief contact with the floor. Circumstances are sometimes such that the natural reaction to rebound or roll from a landing has to be halted. In a restricted situation, where a partner, a wall or apparatus limits the space available, the checking of momentum in a safe way is vital. The flexion on landing has to be followed by a deliberate straightening of the body, which gains the stability of the vertical position.

## Teaching

Flight should occur in every gymnastic lesson whatever the main movement idea. The exhilaration of flight is not gained immediately; to some the feeling of being unsupported in the air is frightening. The teacher, therefore, has a great responsibility. Children can never enjoy gymnastics if they are uneasy in the air, and in such situations the safety of individuals is in doubt.

The elementary stages of flight (see Chapter 3), where bouncing and other activities involving resiliency are stressed, serve a dual purpose. They give the basic experience of leaving and meeting the floor, as well as fostering confidence. As take-offs and landings become more proficient, so the period of flight is increased and only classes well trained in the basic work will be able to exploit the situation.

Advanced flight could be taken with older Juniors or from the second year onwards with Secondary children. When this theme is introduced it would be valuable to review some of the earlier resiliency tasks, for although the stress will be on actions in the air, the longer the flight the more important the preparation and recovery.

### BODY SHAPE DURING FLIGHT

This can be developed from earlier work where parts of the body are emphasised while in the air, but in this situation the whole body is involved in gaining and holding the shape.

The previous experience of moving symmetrically and asymmetrically can be recalled and now investigated in the air. A double take-off will probably lead to a symmetrical shape and a single take-off to a shape with a one-sided stress. It could be an added challenge to achieve asymmetrical flight from a double take-off and vice versa. Through experimenting it will be discovered that a double take-off usually sends the body vertically upwards while a single take-off leads to length of flight. In the latter situation the use of the free leg could be stressed to gain a swinging impetus at take-off or to anticipate the shape to be held.

The teaching points to consider are:

(a) that the whole body participates in the shape, particularly the head, which is often misdirected towards the landing area,
(b) that the shape is held clearly without strain for as long as possible,
(c) that the take-off and landing are not impaired because of the focus on flight.

### OFF-BALANCE FLIGHT

The position of the body in flight is normally vertical or nearly so. This gives a sense of balance and stability despite the loss of contact with the ground. Even when the flight is forward or backward from feet to hands the body still moves in a stable way. Although both the stability of dimensional movement and the unstable or labile state associated with moving in the diagonal are of vital interest to the dancer, the gymnast is mainly concerned with the former but can experience the latter in a limited way.

Tipping the body to lose balance will have been mastered on the floor and on apparatus. Now the aim is to jump into an inclined position. The direction of flight can be diagonally upward or diagonally downward. Since the centre of gravity falls out of line with the rest of the body, off-balance is experienced.

Flight into the diagonal demands the confidence to throw the body off-balance and the ability to land safely. Inevitably the landings are in the nature of a fall, and a quick adjustment and transference of weight are needed if injury is to be avoided and control regained. This work is obviously for those possessing great skill, and can be taken profitably and safely only with classes whose movement experience is considerable. In Secondary schools where gymnastic clubs exist as part of extra-curricular activities, off-balance flight would provide ideal material for able individuals.

All flight situations can be taken as floorwork, but losing balance while in the air can be achieved only when the flight is prolonged. Therefore apparatus which assists take-off is most useful when this theme is explored. Such apparatus is discussed later in this chapter.

### TURNING IN FLIGHT

When a shape is held during flight there is a feeling of pausing or hovering in the air. Turning in the air gives a sense of carrying on the action instead of arresting it.

Turning around the vertical axis during flight is mastered quickly by all children. Quarter, half and three-quarter turns bring about a change of front and are used extensively in floorwork. The run-up is usually forward and at take-off a pivoting action occurs. The arms, and in a one foot take-off the free leg, can add a swinging impetus to the pivot. Juniors often throw themselves upward and around from a standing start. Here the upper part of the body prepares by twisting away from the direction of the turn. It is the explosive release of the twist together with the push of the legs that sends the body up and into a turn. Children should be encouraged to turn to both left and right, and to discover how a single take-off influences the direction of the turn.

After a turn around the vertical axis, the landing is usually on feet or hands and feet, but the act of turning enables weight to be transferred on to other parts easily. A common example of this is a half-turn from a forward run, where rolling backwards naturally follows the landing. Transferring weight after a turn is also a vital safety measure. The body continues to rotate after the landing foot has touched the ground and this foot must be released quickly otherwise ankle and knee are liable to be twisted. Weight could be transferred on to the other foot and then into a series of steps where the turning is continued and allowed to peter out, or on to different parts in succession.

Turning around the side to side axis in flight demands considerable skill. If the starting position is on the feet, a half-turn in the forwards direction on to hands brings about "catspring-like" actions and dive rolls. The teacher will find that these skills, and variations upon them, are within the capabilities of most children. In the beginning stages the hands may be placed before the feet leave the ground thus obviating flight. Although this will be accepted at first the teacher should encourage flight with the idea of springing up and over on to the hands. When the flight is minimal the weight is taken momentarily on to the hands before being pushed back on to the feet. With increased flight the body actually lands on the hands. The teaching points here are that the hands yield on impact, the head is tucked and the back rounded so that a roll results. Some children may be able to flex the arms on landing and use a pushing action to send the body backwards through the air to land on the feet again.

Forward and backward half-turns where the weight is taken on the upper half of the body and then thrown on to the feet can be discovered by experimenting. Recognisable skills such as headsprings and shouldersprings would be produced but the teacher should not set out with a few known actions in mind. In such work the tasks should be worded so that movement ideas are given instead of skills dictated. A few individuals will be able to fly from feet to hands and on to feet continuing in one direction, as in handsprings. Variations can be produced by having a one-sided stress, by altering the trajectory, and in repetitive actions, bringing about a climax. Thus flight occurs into and out of weight on hands and two half-turns are completed.

All children can cope with skills using a spring from the legs but when the take-off is from the upper part of the body few girls can produce an efficient action. This type of body management will therefore form a considerable part of boys' advanced work, where the majority can produce the required strength. Teachers of Secondary girls will recognise the inability of the majority to excel in such work, and although some of these ideas could be taken in a gymnastic club, they do not form material suitable for a normal class lesson.

Complete turning in flight about the side to side axis results in forward and backward somersaults. These can be part of floor work but generally apparatus is used to assist the take-off and prolong the flight. This is another aspect of the work that has a particular appeal to boys. Once forward and backward somersaults have been achieved they can be combined with twisting in stretched or arched positions. Without doubt this work is challenging to skilled gymnasts but it is rarely applicable to the average gymnastic lesson, and so is suggested as material for gymnastic clubs.

Turning around the forward and backward axis during flight brings about cartwheeling in the air. This is a skill that only the exceptional child can achieve, and as such does not enter into teaching gymnastics at class level.

## Apparatus

Apparatus, a partner or a group can assist an individual at one or more of the three flight phases. Partner- and group-assisted flight are discussed in Chapters 9 and 13.

### APPARATUS ASSISTING TAKE-OFF

If the natural spring of the child has been cultivated during the early gymnastic themes the teacher will find that there is an easy transition to apparatus. Unless the basic work has been taught well such apparatus cannot be used effectively. The teacher should realise that springboards and the like are not to be used as a substitute for the performer's own ejecting powers, but as a means of gaining additional impetus at take-off.

The various types of apparatus used to assist take-off can be considered progressively. A form or box top gives a raised "step up" start, as does an inclined plank or storming board, where a run usually precedes the take-off. This type of apparatus does not aid take-off by its construction but by the way it is placed and used. Simple arrangements of such apparatus could provide the link between unassisted take-offs and the use of springboards.

Beating boards give only a little assistance but the many kinds of springboards and twinsprings give considerable impetus when used well. When this apparatus is introduced, probably in the last year in the Junior school or the second year in Secondary school, it is vital that the children are given time to explore its potential. This means that the springboard should be used first in isolation and not given immediately as a means of getting on to a high piece of apparatus. In this situation the children should be encouraged to find the area giving most assistance and to experiment with using one or both feet.

Taking off from a springboard is similar to springing from the floor, the main difference being that the action has to be speeded up considerably. The teaching points are that the stress is on going up out of and not down into the springboard. In addition the body should be in line with the upward thrust gained, so that whether using one or both feet the body must be over the base at take-off.

Trampettes, which give the most assistance at take-off, are becoming standard equipment in many Secondary schools. Because of the elastic attachment of the bed to the frame the "give" is considerable and the whole take-off action slower than when using a springboard. The introductory stages are particularly important, especially with trampettes where the bed is at an angle to the floor. Since the trampette is used sloping towards the performer there is a danger that the novice will be thrown backwards in flight. Although springboards are best used first without any other apparatus, when starting work on trampettes, it is expedient to use an aid that will keep the weight forward.

The following is suggested as one way of introducing take-offs from trampettes.

(a) The performer sits or kneels on the trampette and bounces, getting the feel of the "give" and recoil of the bed.

(b) Small, standing jumps are experienced with a partner who stands in front or to the side of the trampette, holding hands or forearms. After five or six jumps the performer *steps* off.

(c) Following a few repetitive bounces the performer jumps off, the partner keeping contact and assisting the landing.

(d) A hanging rope which touches the front of the trampette or a bar at chest level could be used as the support instead of a partner.

(e) The first free take-off should have a short approach walk, later a run, with only a slight output of energy and always be on to a rope or bar, which will ensure that the weight is brought forward.

As confidence is gained so full use of the trampette will result. The teaching points are that the approach is controlled, that the centre of the bed is used, that there is a forward lean on take-off and that as the body begins the upward movement there is a lessening of tension resulting in a lightly held position or action.

Once efficient use of springboards and trampettes has been achieved, movement ideas which have been explored at ground level can be re-introduced.

(a) Symmetrical and asymmetrical take-offs and flight—it should be noted that most children have a preference, and that a single take-off from a trampette is possible.

(b) Changes of level, direction and speed all occur naturally when using springboards and trampettes and these could be stressed and "played" with.

APPARATUS THAT ASSISTS FLIGHT

Although by definition flight occurs when the body moves unsupported through the air, hanging apparatus and pieces upon which swinging can take place give a sense of being airborne when used well, and so can be considered as assisting flight. Usually the apparatus is gripped by the hands and the body suspended, although other parts can be used on the trapeze and rings. Some children grip easily and can hold themselves away from the apparatus, others hang and have no sensation of moving through the air. This is particularly so of heavily built children. In such situations the teacher should set progressive tasks that give opportunities for practising gripping and holding.

Apparatus—ropes.

Task.—Jump on to the rope, try to get your head and shoulders above your grip, then lower yourself to the ground.

Apparatus—ropes and form.

Task 1.—Whilst standing on a form, grip the rope, push off, swing and return to the form.

Task 2.—Stand on the form, grip and swing on the rope to land on a mat a few feet away.

**Apparatus**—ropes and two forms.

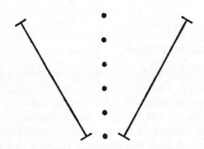

*Task* 1.—Swing from one form to land on the other. The forms are angled so that the children can challenge themselves by selecting a distance relative to their ability.

**Apparatus**—ropes and trampette.

*Task.*—Use a trampette to get high on to a rope, swing and drop off. Here true flight precedes and follows the assisted flight.

Once children can swing easily they enjoy making their own tracks around apparatus arranged as a circuit, where ropes provide the means of getting from one piece to another.

**Apparatus**—a set of ropes, or rings and trapeze, wall bars, inclined form, horse, form narrow side up and box.

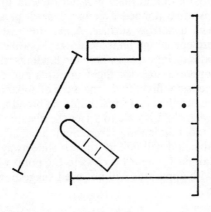

Bars, particularly the narrow metal type, can be used to fly on to and off; the flight can often be boosted by building up the swing on the bar.

## APPARATUS ASSISTING LANDING

When great height has been achieved the landing is usually on to mats or mattresses. The new type of rubber sheeting absorbs the shock of landing far better than fibre mats and does not slip. However, such apparatus cannot give much assistance and it is still necessary for the performer to use his full landing technique. Trampettes can be used for an intermediate landing and in this instance the slope is placed either towards or away from the performer. The jumps will be down from high apparatus and on to the trampette, which will immediately send the body up into the air again and the second landing can be on the floor or another piece of apparatus. In this situation the body does not "give" on contacting the trampette as it would when landing on a firm surface. The ankles flex, but there is only a slight movement of knees and hips, the body being comparatively taut so that the thrust gained from the trampette is transmitted effectively.

## FLIGHT TASKS ON APPARATUS

The teacher should bear several important points in mind when selecting apparatus for flight tasks. Mere height of apparatus does not give a feeling of flight. In a task involving jumping off a high box, few children will go upwards; most will drop, having a sensation of falling, not flying. It would be better to have a low box with a task of jumping on and off. Some pieces have obvious flight associations. It is easy to jump on to and off a box but difficult to jump over. A horizontal bar is often jumped over but it needs great skill to jump and land on such a narrow surface. Apparatus placed high, bars, rings and trapeze encourage jumping upwards, while the placing of mats often dictates or influences where the landings will be made. As well as giving opportunities for flight upwards and downwards the teacher should consider flight from one piece of apparatus to another. In the latter instance the apparatus should be broad and, if possible, angled so that each child is able to select the distance he is to cover. It is important, too, that landings from flight are made on to apparatus which is stable and will neither tip nor slide away.

A teacher who has brought his class to the point where flight can be considered with apparatus will not need suggestions for arrangements and tasks.

The following are given as examples of tasks where flight is considered in relation to other movement ideas.

**Apparatus**—ropes, an angled form, mattress.

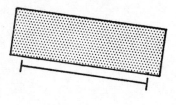

*Task.*—Assisted flight on to the form, off on to the mattress and return to catch the swinging rope arriving back at the start. (Assisted flight, continuity and timing.)

**Apparatus**—springboard angled to box, mats.

*Task.*—Weight on hands to get on to the box, spring off showing a clear shape, land resiliently. (Flight and body shape.)

**Apparatus**—springboard to two boxes of the same height placed lengthways and parallel.

*Task.*—Flight into weight on hands, either going through the gap, legs over or under, or over one box. (Flight with twisting and turning.)

**Apparatus**—ropes, trapeze and rings.

*Task.*—A swinging sequence showing twisting on one piece and turning between two pieces. (Assisted flight with twisting and turning.)

**Apparatus**—trampette to bar or horse or box.

*Task 1.*—From flight arrive on apparatus poised and balanced, any body part to be chosen to take weight. (Flight into balance.)

*Task 2.*—Flight over the apparatus with or without contact. This task could be augmented by

(a) stressing symmetrical or asymmetrical use of the body;
(b) limiting the weight bearing to one or both hands;
(c) dictating the pathway of the body; over, through or to the side of the hand or hands.

It must be stressed that because flight is a vital part of gymnastics it needs to be taught well. Experience and confidence should be built up over the years so that when advanced work is tackled the children are able to enjoy flight and to work safely.

# CHAPTER 13

# GROUP WORK

THIS is a progression from partner work, a group being composed of three or more children. The aim is to explore the gymnastic possibilities of working with others. The benefits and values of group work are similar to those of partner work but the opportunity of working with and adapting to several with mixed abilities and different movement preferences is increased.

The gymnastic group does not have the same relationship as the group in dance. In the latter the group situation can be fully developed but the gymnastic group comes together solely to accomplish a task. It is a working unit held together by a common aim.

## *Material*

All the partner situations can be investigated by the group, as well as new possibilities, because of the greater number of participants.

### 1. COPYING PART OR WHOLE OF A SEQUENCE

This can be tackled by a small group but it is limiting on the floor except when following tracks. On apparatus such tasks can be most challenging to skilled performers, but are not suitable where the ability range within the group is great.

### 2. MAKING AND NEGOTIATING OBSTACLES

This is an ideal starting point for a small group on the floor. One can provide an obstacle for the rest of the group to negotiate in turn. Two of the group can combine to make an obstacle or provide two separate obstacles. When each child makes and negotiates an obstacle in turn, split second timing is demanded within the group.

### 3. MATCHING ACTIONS

In a threesome such challenges can be met by all moving together. In groups of four or more the matching is usually achieved in canon, particularly on apparatus.

### 4. TAKING ALL OR PART OF ONE PERSON'S WEIGHT

This idea can be developed considerably by a group.

*Balancing.*—One can balance on two. In the early stages the two should be at the same level; later, the child who is balancing can be presented with two different levels. When stable balances have been achieved, the two supporters can help the performer into the balance position, tip him off balance and help him recover afterwards.

*Lifting, carrying and lowering.*—This is a situation to be exploited in group work. One child can only bear his partner's weight for a short time but within a group one person can be lifted and carried a considerable distance before being lowered. It is important that the carrying should have some objective. The aim could be to carry a child from one piece of apparatus to another, help him on to a high piece of apparatus, or to lift him from an inversion, change his position during the carrying and place him upright on the floor.

*Flight.*—As one person can help another in all stages of flight so can a group help one of its number. Here again the help should be considerable compared with the partner situation, and prolonged flight as well as catching (instead of assisted landing) could develop.

*Counter-tension.*—Three, or at the most four, children can work together with counter-tension. This is best carried out on apparatus and is usually associated with lifting and lowering.

In group work, although one situation is pursued in the beginning stages, thereafter on being challenged or given a starting point the children will tend to include more than one way of working.

With an increase in the number of people working together it is possible to handle not only each other but also apparatus. The idea of a group manipulating apparatus is dealt with in the apparatus section.

### Teaching

There is no doubt that when children have acquired a certain degree of skill they enjoy working with others and gain much satisfaction from the results. However, this is advanced work and enjoyment and satisfaction will come only if the children feel safe in the group situation. Confidence and safety stem from the mastery of the body and movement understanding. Situations in which children work together and are responsible for each other must be introduced carefully and the teacher should see that all the precautions given under partner work are considered.

The size of the group influences the way in which it acts. This is an important factor when the teacher is deciding how to divide a class and what challenges to set. Three children will work together much as in the partner situation, occasionally dividing into two, who match or support, and one, who is lifted or ejected. A foursome will either work as a matching group or split into two interchangeable pairs. A group of five will only occasionally work identically; they will tend to split into a two and a three, or four will help one, as in carrying or catching after flight. A group of six will usually divide into three couples or two threesomes, changing between these. Groups of more than six are unwieldy, and the most profitable group work seems to come from units of three, four or five.

The children working in groups will have had at least three or four years' gymnastic experience and the teacher will find that his role changes as the work progresses. At the introductory stage he may need to set definite tasks, offer suggestions and help them to see how certain situations could be developed. Very soon, however, the groups will become self-sufficient. They challenge themselves, have many ideas from which to select and are generally independent. At this stage the teacher is more of an adviser, helping the group to clarify ideas, seeing that there is a give and take and not allowing one child always to dictate. Although leaders, in the sense that they are most forthcoming in ideas, will emerge, it is interesting to note that these are not necessarily skilled performers but children of varying abilities.

As in partner work, the teacher can anticipate certain happenings during the exploratory stages of group work. These are: an initial deterioration of an individual's movement, much discussion, the need for a long working time and the tendency to string together ideas or contrive situations.

If the children have been well taught the teacher will see in their final group sequences the fusion of most of their previous work.

Group work can be introduced by giving simple tasks without apparatus; the following are suitable for groups of three;

*Task* 1.—Find ways in which two can assist one to achieve flight.
*Task* 2.—Experiment with gaining and losing counter-tension positions.
*Task* 3.—Two provide different bases for one to use for balance.
*Task* 4.—Two make an obstacle for one to negotiate with or without contact.

### *Apparatus*

The group situation is best explored on apparatus. To introduce the idea the teacher could give each group a variety of apparatus well spaced, and set tasks which involve an awareness of others working.

N

**Apparatus**—double bars, wall bars, two forms, box and three mats to form a large circuit.

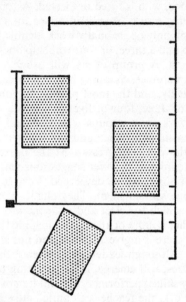

*Task* 1.—Group of 3 to 6.

All start at different points on the apparatus. Choose your own pathway and by adjusting your actions, speed and direction, avoid getting in each other's way.

*Task* 2.—Group of 3 to 6.

Work as before, but instead of taking avoiding action when your pathways cross, go over or under each other (moving obstacles).

For progression fewer pieces of apparatus should be used with less space and a specific group task given.

**Apparatus**—ropes and bars.

*Task.*—Group of 3 to 6.

Matching actions to arrive on and leave the bars, either simultaneously or in canon.

**Apparatus**—window ladder or hinged frame.

*Task.*—Group of 3 to 6.

Matching actions to ascend and descend. This would result in a pattern-stressed sequence.

**Apparatus**—box or horse.

*Task.*—Group of 3.

Get on, off and over, singly and together.

**Apparatus**—horse over form.

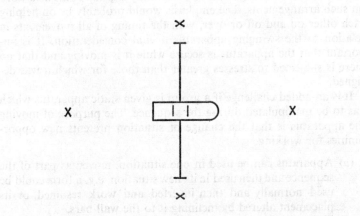

*Task.*—Group of 4.

Start at the points indicated and work towards the horse, passing each other by going over and under.

**Apparatus**—bar box or buck.

*Task.*—Group of 3.

Arrive on and leave by means of counter-tension, lifting or lowering.

**Apparatus**—low box or buck.

*Task.*—Group of 3.

Each one in turn to be helped over the apparatus by assisted flight.

**Apparatus**—trampette surrounded by mats.

*Task.*—Group of 3 or 4.

Invent a rhythmical sequence of jumps on to and off the trampette.

Once groups have perfected sequences on teacher-selected arrangements they will be ready to choose their own apparatus and to set their own tasks.

## GROUP WORK ON APPARATUS THAT MOVES OR IS MOVED

The use of mobile apparatus is mentioned in the chapter on Advanced Body Management and obviously a group could also work on such arrangements. The emphasis would probably be on helping each other on and off or over, with the timing of all movements in relation to the swinging apparatus a vital consideration. It is important that the apparatus is secure while it is moving and that no piece is subjected to stresses greater than those for which it was designed.

It is an added challenge if a group is given static apparatus which has to be manipulated during the sequence. The purpose of moving the apparatus is that the change of situation presents new opportunities for working.

(a) Apparatus can be used in one situation, moved as part of the sequence and then used in its new situation, e.g. a form could be used normally and then inverted and work resumed, or its placement altered by inclining it to the wall bars.

(b) The apparatus could be held in its new situation by some of the group whilst the rest work on it, e.g. a form could be held away from the ground and used as an obstacle to get over, with or without contact.

(c) The apparatus could be used by one child while the rest of the group move it, e.g. a form or box top can be lifted or tilted while one person maintains a balance on it.

The moving of any apparatus should be an integral part of the group's sequence.

This work is undoubtedly exciting to children whose gymnastic experience is wide since it demands a high degree of co-operation, inventiveness and skill. Some groups will tend to produce artificial situations in the beginning stages but the teacher can do much to guide them towards logical, well-developed work.

Group work and mobile apparatus are comparatively new developments in gymnastics. As the work progresses and the capabilities of children are realised, it is inevitable that new apparatus must be designed. The teacher can augment his traditional apparatus by unusual arrangements and by joining pieces imaginatively, provided that the apparatus is completely safe when used in an unorthodox way.

CHAPTER 14

# SYLLABUS AND PROGRESSIONS

THIS book deals with the Junior and Secondary age groups but it is of value to look briefly at what the child does at Nursery and Infant level. In the Nursery school and reception class the child should have a rich variety of movement experience, including climbing on apparatus and manipulating objects of different shapes and sizes. This scrambling on apparatus is not yet gymnastics in the accepted sense but movement play. In the Infant school most children can work on simple challenges which are aimed at widening their movement vocabulary. In answering given tasks the process of choosing involves a conscious physical and mental effort and this is the beginning of gymnastics.

The Junior level should surely be the "age of gymnastics." The characteristics of Juniors—their liveliness, boundless energy and the intent with which they set about learning new skills—makes them "ripe" for objective work. Their love of daring, their need for adventure and new experiences all point to the suitability of gymnastics at this age.

For Secondary girls gymnastics should continue for the first two or three years, provided that the movement experience in the Junior school has been a rich one. Thereafter although movement education must be continued in some form, gymnastics could become an optional activity. Boys, because of their superior strength and a need to prove themselves physically, could pursue gymnastics further, so that a choice after the fourth year would be more appropriate. The majority of children who have been taught well for six years will have reached a point, physically, where further work becomes a matter of permutations and combinations both of action and apparatus. There will be a minority, however, who prefer gymnastics to any other form of physical activity and they should be given the opportunity to master further skills.

Those who opt for gymnastics could continue with some of the advanced aspects of flight or balance, for example, which cannot be dealt with in the normal class situation. These activities on the whole are for the few, and therefore should be taken only where the educational considerations of catering for all no longer exist. The skills involved in rebound tumbling could be mastered. This is not referred to in this book although the actions are gymnastic. Undoubtedly trampolining and gymnastics are allied skills, co-ordination, control

## TABLE I

|  | JUNIOR | | | | SECONDARY | | |
|---|---|---|---|---|---|---|---|
|  | 7–8 years | 8–9 years | 9–10 years | 10–11 years | 11–12 years | 12–13 years | 13–14 years |
|  | Locomotion, Stillness, Weight bearing } Elementary Body Management | Weight bearing, Weight transference, Control of body weight } Elementary body management | Stretching and curling, Twisting and turning, Control of tension } Intermediate body management | Symmetry, Asymmetry } Intermediate body management | Advanced flight | Body shape—Space | Advanced body management |
|  | Pathways, Direction } Space | Direction, Level } Space | Acceleration, Deceleration } Speed | Balance, Control of tension, Flight, Control of energy, Continuity | Advanced balance | Rhythm, Climax } Speed | Mobile apparatus |
|  |  | Quick, Slow } Speed | Continuity | Partner Work: (4) Matching (5) Moving obstacles | Rhythm, Climax } Speed | Partner Work: (7) Lifting and lowering (8) Counter-balance counter-tension | Group work |
|  |  |  | Partner Work: (1) Following pathways (2) Copying (3) Obstacles |  | Partner Work: (6) Taking all or part of partner's weight | Group work |  |
|  |  |  |  |  | Work in threes |  |  |

TABLE II

| 11–12 years | 12–13 years | 13–14 years | 14–15 years | 15–16 years |
|---|---|---|---|---|
| Locomotion<br>Stillness<br>Weight bearing<br>Weight transference } Elementary body management | Symmetry and Asymmetry } Intermediate Body Management | Balance<br>Flight | Advanced flight<br>Advanced balance | Mobile apparatus |
| Stretching and curling<br>Twisting and turning } Intermediate body management | Acceleration<br>Deceleration } Speed | Continuity | Body shape—Space | Work in threes |
| Control of body weight<br>Pathways<br>Direction } Space<br>Levels | Continuity | Advanced body management | Rhythm } Speed<br>Climax | Group work |
| Quick } Speed<br>Slow | Balance<br>Control of tension<br>Flight<br>Control of energy<br>Partner work:<br>(1) Following pathways<br>(2) Copying<br>(3) Obstacles | Rhythm } Speed<br>Climax<br>Partner work:<br>(4) Matching<br>(5) Moving obstacles<br>(6) Taking all or part of partner's weight<br>Work in threes | Partner work:<br>(7) Lifting and lowering<br>(8) Counter-balance counter-tension<br>Group work | |

and skill being required in both, but a piece of apparatus so extravagant of space and time, and usually limited to the use of one person, cannot be contemplated in a normal lesson and is better kept either for a small group or included as an out-of-school activity.

It is increasingly evident that as the scope of Physical Education widens it is advisable to allow a certain freedom of choice once a variety of activities has been introduced and developed to the extent where a selection can be made. This is often limited by space and staff but in most schools a slight degree of choice can be offered.

The plan shown in Table I is meant to be used as a guide and is an outline based on one gymnastic lesson a week throughout the year. A chronological division has been used as a basis but it is appreciated that this is only one factor to be considered in the development of the child. Although a certain progression is suggested it must be left to the discretion of the teacher when each movement idea is introduced, the length of time spent on each theme and the link between past and present work. Junior teachers will probably realise that if classes have had good teaching throughout the first three years and adequate opportunity to work on suitable apparatus, some of the more advanced work could be explored. Often the ability of Junior classes is underestimated, and if these children are to be fully extended and their potential reached, then some of the more difficult work must be covered.

If the Secondary intake is from Junior schools where the children have had little or no gymnastic experience then the work must be condensed. It will be obvious from both the text and from Table II that this is far from ideal. The elementary body management ideas which have to be covered when the child is eleven to twelve years of age must be tackled differently. The children are past the stage when some of these ideas are interesting and stimulating and relate to their natural ways of moving. The work must now be taken out of context and many situations may become artificial unless the teacher is aware of the stage of development reached by any age group.

# CHAPTER 15

# CONCLUSION

ALTHOUGH the method of teaching gymnastics advocated in this book has been in existence for well over ten years, it is far from being fully developed.

The need and place of Physical Education in the school curriculum are still not generally accepted. Facilities and equipment, however, are gradually improving. For many years Junior schools have had totally inadequate apparatus with which to challenge lively, energetic, adventurous and often skilful individuals. Gradually this is being remedied by progressive Authorities, and climbing frames, ropes, bars and storming boards, as well as the traditional portable apparatus previously "saved" for the Secondary school, are being installed. Space, too, is restricted and although some schools have halls, often the playground is the only area available for gymnastics. This also is slowly being rectified and the plans for new schools usually include a space suitable for physical activity. Perhaps the time will come when fully equipped gymnasia will be recognised as a necessary provision in all Junior schools.

In Secondary schools the conventional horse, buck and box are being supplemented by new, more exciting and adaptable pieces, while combinations of fixed apparatus such as is found in the Cave Southampton, where bars, ropes and window ladders are related, provide a more versatile arrangement.

Experiments have been made not only with lighter materials but also with new pieces of apparatus such as trolleys, which are designed specifically to be used while moving. Teachers and manufacturers of gymnastic equipment should realise the need for apparatus which meets the growing demands of this work. Gymnastics as it is taught today cannot continue to develop with apparatus designed for a different system.

The standard of teaching improves yearly; more students are being introduced to this method of teaching, while a greater number of them start their training with some previous personal experience of modern work. Although most Colleges of Education provide a professional course for all students, some still limit their main subject course to those training to teach in the Secondary school. If, as is indicated in this book, it is in the Junior school that the bulk of the work is taught, then surely Primary teachers should not be excluded from a main course of study.

It will be appreciated, therefore, that even though equipment, facilities and training have all contributed towards the general raising of the standard of gymnastic teaching, much has still to be done.

# INDEX

*Page numbers giving definition are shown in bold type*